Part I:

The English Version

Are

Your

Health and Finances

Linked?

A Christian Entrepreneur's Quest

Ruth Wuwong

Are Your Health and Finances Linked?

Disclaimer Notice:

Please note the information contained within this document is for educational and entertainment purposes only. All effort has been executed to present accurate, up-to-date, reliable, complete information. No warranties of any kind are declared or implied. Readers acknowledge the author is not engaged in the rendering of legal, financial, medical, or professional advice.
Under no circumstances will any blame or legal responsibility be held against the author for any damages, reparation, or monetary loss because of the information in this booklet directly or indirectly.

Unless otherwise noted, all Scripture taken from the New International Version.

ISBN: 979-8-88904-004-0

Published by Vidasym Publishing
A Division of Vidasym, Inc.
5013 S. Louis Ave., #532
Sioux Falls, SD 57108

Content

DEDICATION

I dedicate this book foremost to my Savior,
the Lord Jesus Christ.

Furthermore, I dedicate this book to my friends
who have supported us
in our ministry over the years.

FOREWORD

Who doesn't want to be successful in managing their health and finances? Christians are called to care about both. In this booklet, Ruth Wuwong provides valuable and practical advice based on her life experience and converts many of her lessons learned into habits that can be adopted to improve one's health and financial well-being. Ruth details her faith journey and its impact on critical decisions that have helped, by God's grace, to bring her and her husband Ken good health and financial security.

(Dr. Terry Opgenorth worked at Abbott Laboratories' Pharma division (now AbbVie) as scientist and executive for 20 years. After Abbott, he served as CEO of Vidasym, a start-up biotech company, and was a co-founder of VetDC, a veterinary oncology company.)

AMAZON REVIEWS

Since its publication in 12/2022, this booklet has received 42 favorable reviews in 9 months. A recent Amazon verified purchase review is shown below.

"This is the second book I read from this author; I like her writing style because it is very practical. I see this book as two books in one, which I really like. The first part is about how to maintain and improve good health and the second part is about money. As the author said: "making money is important, but how to manage what you have is even more critical." My favorite chapter was the one about stock and asset allocation. I like that the author explains the concepts in an easy-to-understand way and after reading that chapter I realized that buying stocks is not as complicated as I thought, and that is something I actually can do. I highly recommend this book to anyone who wants to improve their health and finances."

Chapter 1: Introduction

While I was a graduate student at Ohio State University, Lily took care of me like her own sister. Although Covid-19 still prevented people from traveling freely, I told my husband Ken, "Lily is in her eighties. We ought to make a special trip to see her."

A visit to this old friend brought back many recollections, some painful, some sweet. During our time together, Lily talked about our shared past. "I remember your father passed away when you were sixteen. Your mother once mentioned to me you have a bad family history of high cholesterol, diabetes, and weight issues. I noticed your mother was overweight and had diabetes. Back then, even at the tender age of twenty, you appeared rather chubby."

She grasped my hand, her lips curling into a grin. "Look at you now. You're in your late sixties, right? You're slim and robust. What did you do to overcome your genetic predispositions, even when the statistics aren't in your favor? You should share your tips. I'm sure others will benefit from them."

Her words triggered such intense emotions that I became tongue-tied. Memories of my entire lifetime crashed over me, leaving one truth in their wake—God has guided us through insurmountable challenges to reach our current status, not only with my health but also with wealth and good relationships.

My husband, Ken, is a retired pastor, and together, he and I served counseled quite a few couples, and I made an interesting observation. Financial anxieties hurt health and relationships. The reverse is also true. Poor relationships affect people's well-being and prevent them from pursuing their dreams, and illness disrupts marriage and a person's pursuit of financial independence. Health, wealth, and relationships intertwine so intimately that it is difficult to single any of them out.

No, we aren't wealthy like Bill Gates or Warren Buffett, but have achieved financial independence. When we got married, the combined dollar amount in our checking account was less than fifty dollars. Yet we've come a long way! We can retire early on our own terms and donate sizeable sums of money to selected nonprofit organizations.

In the following chapters, I hope my shared stories will help you improve your health and wealth.

Chapter 2: My Body, My Health

If one million—1,000,000—represents your life, your health is the number **One** that is followed by many zeros, with each zero representing one of your treasured things. Without that One, all those zeros amount to nothing.

We all know health is important. Many of us spend money and effort trying to maintain our well-being: avoid tobacco/drug usage, reduce alcohol intake, build our diet around healthy choices, exercise, get enough sleep… The list can be long.

But how do we define good health? If I don't have any disease or infirmity, am I considered a healthy person?

Although different definitions have been used to define "health" for distinct purposes, information from the World Health Organization (WHO) shows that health is a state of complete physical, mental, and social well-being and not merely the absence of disease and infirmity. Furthermore, health is a positive concept emphasizing social and personal resources, as well as physical capacities.

Data from the Centers for Disease Control and Prevention (CDC) show that healthcare costs in the United States were $3.5 trillion in 2017. Yet we have a lower life expectancy than people in other developed countries.

Why?

There are no straightforward answers.

Ruth Wuwong

Although physical condition comes to mind automatically when we mention the word *health*, spiritual, relational, and financial aspects are equally important. Many studies have shown these different components intertwine and affect one another in a profound way.

For example, people with better relationships have a larger capacity to handle hardship and suffering and achieve better emotional balance. Those with good spiritual health may feel a sense of calm and purpose that drives them to achieve harmony in other aspects of life.

So, what contributes to good physical health? The cliché response is to establish healthy habits in your diet, exercise, and sleep.

My stories begin with a question that seeks a quick response, but unfortunately, there is no such thing as an easy answer. Read on to find out how I came up with workable solutions for my health issues.

Chapter 3: Establish Healthy Habits

Most of us brush our teeth every day. How did we form that habit? Likely, our parents imposed it on us before we learned that teeth brushing is important for maintaining oral hygiene.

We all know diet and exercise are crucial for better physical health. Yet, why do many of us find it difficult to eat right and exercise every day? Why can't we make them as easy as brushing our teeth?

In my early forties, an annual physical checkup revealed I had high cholesterol and that my HbA1c (a measure of average blood glucose sugar levels for the last two to three months) trended high.

My doctor advised me to change my eating habit and lose weight. "Do you exercise regularly? A combination of exercise and diet will help." Then she sent me to a dietitian.

I still remember the dietitian's earnest countenance when she stared into my eyes. "You can't eat out anymore. When you cook your meals, avoid meat and seafood high in cholesterol such as shrimp and squid."

Her words spiraled my spirit into despair, for I love food. My husband would often joke that I thought about what to eat for dinner right after I finished lunch.

During the previous twenty years, my life had formed a routine that seemed to serve me well. How could I alter it?

The answer stared back at me—my routine didn't work anymore.

cholesterol and diabetes would wreck my health. My father died young, so I didn't know whether he'd developed hyperlipidemia. But all my uncles and aunts suffered dire consequences such as stroke or heart attack from high cholesterol. On my mother's side, complications associated with obesity and diabetes killed my grandfather and one of her siblings. My mom was also overweight and diabetic. Eventually, she passed away from a diabetes-induced stroke.

Yet, what could I do to change my diet and start exercising?

As a scientist with a PhD in biochemistry, I approach everything by first conducting thorough research. I tried to learn as much as I could about diet and exercise and found something interesting: Most people fail because they don't realize that the only way to eat right and exercise consistently is to turn them into habits. For example, once you form the habit of exercise, and it becomes like brushing your teeth in the morning, you'll have a better chance of adhering to it.

So, I delved deeper into the subject of how to form a habit.

Some of you may have heard about the 21-day habit formation formula. However, according to Dr. Phillippa Lally, a health psychology researcher at University College London, a new habit may take over two months to take shape and more than eight months to become fully formed.

No wonder it's so challenging for us to establish an exercise routine.

In his book, *The Power of Habit*, Charles Duhigg attributes the formation of habits to a psychological pattern called the "habit loop"—the trigger (or cue), the routine, and the reward.

Studies have shown that an effective way to shift a habit is to discover and keep your old cue and reward and change only the routine.

From my personal experiences, I concur with that approach.

First, I dissected my daily routine.

For years, I have been following the No-B-No-B (No-Bible-No-Breakfast) practice for my daily devotion. Here is the cue-routine-reward loop associated with that habit.

Cue: My alarm goes off at 6 a.m.

Routine: I get up, brush my teeth, wash my face, and then do my morning devotion.

Reward: I'm mentally calm and prepared to start a new day.

Also, now I get to eat my breakfast.

What should I do to modify my routine and to keep the same cue and reward?

Now, please note another word of caution: **DO NOT** try to change your routine all at once. Instead, take baby steps to insert small, achievable activities into that routine. Otherwise, you're doomed to fail.

After some consideration, I added ten simple sit-ups following my prayer.

Good gracious, not as easy as I thought!

In my hurry to get to breakfast and dash out of the door for work, I had to force myself to get it done. As time went by, the new mini-habit stuck, and I added additional stretch exercises and even foot massage (reflexology: see Chapter 4 for more information). In all, I only added ten more minutes to my routine. I have been doing this for 20+ years and truly benefit from my habitual morning exercise.

Yet I needed thirty minutes of exercise each day, including a good cardiovascular workout.

Back to Square One. I observed that after work, I picked up my son from school, went home, and then took a shower as if to wash away all my anxieties and worries brought on by my job.

Here is another cue-routine-reward loop associated with that habit.

Cue: I get home and drop my purse on the sofa.

Routine: I take a shower.

Reward: I feel refreshed and ready to cook dinner.

Could I exercise before taking a shower? Why not?

Again, I started small. From an extensive online search, I concluded that rope-jumping, which does not require a lot of space and investment, should be something to try. Plus, it offers numerous other benefits. Besides providing an efficient cardio workout, it also enhances balance and agility and boosts bone density.

On the first day, I jumped ten times and was already huffing and puffing as if I'd just run a marathon. Well, I had not skipped rope since middle school. I decided on the spot to cut it down and jump only five times. From that humble beginning, things got better. Still, it took me an entire year to increase to 300 times. Later, I broke the 300 times into five cycles and added stretching and weight-lifting in

In essence, I added only twenty more minutes to my routine and have gained tremendous benefits. I reached the goal of bringing my body mass index (BMI) into the standard range. Not only do I feel stronger and more energetic, but I have been maintaining the same BMI for the past two decades.

Enough about exercise. How about food—an entirely different beast?

As mentioned above, I love food. I've tried dieting to no avail. When I'm hungry, I tend to eat whatever I can get my hands on. After reflecting on my eating habit, I decided to eat more often in small portions. In other words, avoid getting into a food-craving state at all costs.

I discovered that besides three meals, my daily routine involved two coffee breaks, one in the morning at around 10 a.m. and the other at 3 p.m.

Here is the cue-routine-reward loop associated with that habit.

Cue: I glance at my watch. 10 a.m. Time for my coffee break.

Routine: I get up, grab a cup of coffee, and then snatch a piece of whatever sweets provided by my company on that day.

Reward: I feel relaxed, satisfied, and ready to get back to work.

Should I bring my own healthier choices and enjoy them during the coffee break?

So, I maintained the same cue/reward and replaced the routine with an apple or a banana instead of sweets. Gradually, I establish my current habit of eating six times a day.

Breakfast (around 7 a.m.): low carbs like a 1/2 cup serving of cottage cheese, or one medium avocado, or a cup of smoothie made from veggies and fruits.

Mid-morning snack (around 10 a.m.): fruit or yogurt.

Lunch (around noon): some carbs like noodles or pasta, plus an egg and vegetables.

Mid-afternoon snack (around 3 p.m.): fruit or yogurt.

Dinner (around 6 p.m.): no carbs, meat and vegetables only.

Night-time snack (around 9 p.m.): fruit.

By eating frequent small portions, my blood glucose and insulin levels won't spike and fall into a wild pattern. My mother developed full-blown diabetes in her forties. As of today (in my late sixties), I have managed to fend it off. I believe weight control, diet, exercise

Another reminder: Avoid processed food. If possible, try to make everything from scratch, which is healthier and more economical.

As mentioned above, I often eat cottage cheese for breakfast, but it's plain, almost tasteless. To make it more appetizing, I used to mix jam into it, even though commercially prepared jam contains a high percentage of added sugars.

Could I replace the jam from the store with something homemade?

At the end of one summer, I found hundreds of unripe fruits on the cherry tomato vines in my garden.

Should I dump them? What a waste.

After some research, I made them into a smoothie, then boiled it with sugar and maltose (for thickening). The product? A homemade green sauce perfect for my cottage cheese. Since I added little sugar with no preservatives, I froze them into small Ziplock bags and thawed one bag each week. If you're interested in the recipe, drop me a note, and I'll send it to you.

So far, I have only talked about good habits. What about if you have bad habits such as smoking, drugs, or alcohol? Can you break unhealthy habits by following the same cue-routine-reward loop?

Yes, and no. Some problems require professional help and are beyond the scope of this book.

I do recommend, if possible, joining an accountability group.

For several months, I belonged to an accountability group at our church. The four of us, all women, met once a week.

Initially, we focused on reporting what we did during the past week, including whether we read our Bible daily, exercised, and ate a healthy diet. The sharing helped us recognize our bad habits, and we encouraged one another to establish healthy ones.

Our small group soon morphed beyond health issues. When we grew more intimate, we shared our problems concerning work, spouses, children, etc. One of the sisters back then faced a dilemma: whether to pursue her PhD degree in theology. With the help of the accountability group, she reached her decision. A few weeks ago, she sent me a message to thank me for my encouragement and informed me she is now a Doctor of Old Testament Theology and a regular speaker at various events.

I hope my sharing convinces you it's possible to form a daily habit of eating right and exercising. You may even go beyond that and

Chapter 4: Reflexology and the Benefits of Foot Massage

As a biochemist trained in the Western scientific tradition, I used to object to anything related to Chinese medicine and alternative healing, until a trip to Shanghai changed my perspective.

During a visit to our family in Hong Kong a few years ago, we detoured to mainland China, which had just opened to tourists. While our tour group went to Shanghai, one of my teeth began to give me trouble. The pain became more intolerable by the minute. To our surprise, a sign advertised that a doctor specializing in reflexology resided within our hotel.

"I'll give it a try," I muttered to Ken, gritting my teeth in agony. "It can't get any worse, anyway."

I entered the doctor's office and caught sight of a large, middle-aged woman sitting alone. She gave me a questioning glance but didn't utter a word.

"I—I—" I spoke in Mandarin and grimaced with wry amusement, feeling foolish.

"Can I help you?" Her voice was gentle, unlike her impressive frame.

I swallowed my embarrassment. "I'm here for my toothache."

She gestured for me to take a seat. "Please remove your shoes and socks."

I did as she commanded. She wiped my right foot thoroughly with paused and raised her head. "You had bronchitis recently?"

My jaw almost dropped to the floor. *How did she know?*

She moved to my other foot. After a moment, she looked at me again. "You have a diabetic family background."

I couldn't control my curiosity anymore. "You can tell from examining my feet?"

"Yes." She uttered one simple response and went back to work. "Which tooth is giving you trouble?"

I opened my mouth and pointed to the culprit.

She nodded. "Be prepared. As I press hard on one of your toes, it'll hurt like crazy, but your toothache will subside."

Serious doubts crept into my mind. Then she pushed down on the second toe of my right foot, and I almost jumped up from the chair.

"How does your tooth feel?" she asked in a calm and kind tone.

Tears gathered behind my eyelids. I didn't know if the pain in my toe distracted me or if my toothache had disappeared. "It worked."

"Good. The pain will return, though. Next time when it starts, just massage this point." She showed me the exact spot on my toe. "By the way, you can delay the onset of diabetes by pressing here." She pointed to a small area on my sole.

I walked out of her office, bewilderment bubbling up in my heart. As I entered our room, I couldn't help blurting out, "Ken, you wouldn't believe what I've experienced."

After I told him the story, he shook his head. "I don't believe it. It sounds like magic."

I crossed my arms. "Why don't you go check it out yourself?"

"But I'm not sick." He scratched his head. "Did you say it only cost twenty Chinese yuan? Well, that's not even five US dollars. I'll go."

Thirty minutes later, Ken returned with a disbelieving expression on his face. "She studied my feet and told me I had appendicitis before. She also asked me why I wanted to see her since my health is excellent."

Astonishing, isn't it? Do a Google search, and you'll find over 485,000,000 results on this subject. You can easily purchase a simple foot massage tool for a few bucks. Some books give elaborate illustrations about where to massage, etc. I think the simplest way is to massage your whole foot, bottom, top, and toes. If you make it too it a daily habit.

Since my encounter with that amazing doctor, I've been massaging my feet every morning. My mother had her diabetic onset in her forties. I passed that age more than two decades ago and still haven't developed diabetes. Maybe foot massage does delay the onset of that horrid disease.

Chapter 5: Vitamin D

Have you seen the article entitled "How Vitamin D Affects Omicron Symptoms?" If interested, please drop me a note on my website, www.ruthforchrist.com, and I'll send you the report.

Here is a paragraph from that commentary:

"There may be an association of low vitamin D levels correlated with severe diseases, COVID-19 included. But if there is an immune-boosting benefit to be had, 'it is with standard, low doses and not large doses,' Dr. Spearman clarifies."

About twenty years ago, I started to conduct research in the vitamin D field and quickly learned that my daily intake of 400 IU of vitamin D wasn't sufficient. So, I increased it to 1000 IU a day.

Imagine my shock when my doctor told me I was vitamin D deficient. I didn't have any symptoms other than that my joints hurt sometimes, and I was prone to mild colds. My doctor gave me a prescription for a mega 50,000 IU dose. I took the prescription from her but didn't fill it. Why? Because I knew the hypercalcemic side effect of vitamin D overdose would be detrimental to my body. Instead, I raised my daily intake to 2000 IU. It worked. My vitamin D level went back to normal, and I no longer suffered from joint pain and frequent mild cold.

Is vitamin D a vitamin?

Most people may respond, "Of course."

Many of us know that vitamin D is made in the skin after exposure to sunshine. But the initial form is inactive. It needs to be chemically changed in the liver and kidney in order to become the active form, calcitriol.

Like estrogen or androgen, calcitriol is a hormone that binds to a nuclear receptor, the vitamin D receptor (VDR). Once bound, calcitriol activates VDR to regulate over 200 target genes.

The fact that vitamin D is essential for bone health is well known. Additional evidence suggests that VDR plays an important role in modulating cardiovascular, immunological, metabolic, and other functions. For example, data from epidemiological, preclinical, and clinical studies show that vitamin D deficiency is associated with an increased risk for cardiovascular disease.

Thus, the benefits of vitamin D go beyond building and maintaining strong bones and teeth. To improve your overall health, remember to take 2000 IU of vitamin D every day.

Chapter 6: Stress and Lack of Sleep

Stress can wreak havoc on your mind and body, affecting your sleep, diet, or even your exercise routine. Some specific events in life, such as moving to a new place, changing jobs, or losing a loved one, often lead to increased stress. In our daily routine, do we also experience stress? How do we recognize it?

Several years ago, I worked as a project manager for a major pharmaceutical company. My workload increased bit by bit. Soon, I kept thinking about my job even at night and developed insomnia. My body needed rest, but my mind didn't want to cooperate. I tossed and turned like the sea. Yet no matter how hard I tried, I couldn't sleep. Then the morning came, and I still had to drag my sleep-deprived body to work.

If you have ever experienced sleepless nights, you know how awful it is.

Information from the American Academy of Sleep Medicine website shows that about a third of Americans suffer from periodic insomnia. When you have difficulty sleeping for more than a month, it turns into a chronic condition. One in ten of us may have this chronic disorder and require treatment.

Many factors (e.g., aging, caffeine, pain, medications, apnea, and stress) contribute to insomnia. Stress affects sleep. On the other hand, insomnia also causes stress. It's a vicious cycle.

I asked several people, "What should I do?"

"Quit your job," one woman from my church quipped.

Sorry, not an option.

Another Christian gave me a hard glance. "Have more faith. Pray and leave everything to the Lord."

A friend suggested, "Drink a glass of wine in the evening. It'll make you sleepy."

I did an online search and learned that alcohol may make you feel sleepy at first. But as the alcohol is metabolized, it'll disrupt your sleep. A study shows two drinks for men and one drink for women can decrease sleep quality by 24 percent.

I considered asking my doctor for sleeping pills. With three decades of experiences in the pharmaceutical industry, defaulting to medication seemed an easy way out. Yet, after suffering unwanted effects from certain drugs for years (see Chapter 8 for more information), I've developed a unique concept: Unless it's absolutely necessary, avoid medications.

One day during my morning devotion, I brought my problem to the Lord again, and an idea popped into my mind. "Find a hobby that lets you use your hands, not your brain."

Ah, that was exactly what I needed.

After investigating different hobbies, I settled on jewelry making, mainly because it didn't require a lot of space. I went to a community college to take a course. Every evening at around nine o'clock, I pushed aside my work and focused on my crafts. Amazingly, when I kept my hands busy, my mind automatically relaxed. In a short while, I overcame my insomnia.

Besides having a hobby, other approaches such as exercise, meditation, yoga, massage, etc. can all help reduce stress. However, inactive ways of passing time, such as watching television or surfing the internet, may increase your stress level over the long run.

So, focus on using active methods to manage your stress.

Regarding how to build a better sleep habit, you can find numerous helpful articles by researching the subject on the internet. Follow the cue-routine-reward approach I discussed in Chapter 3, and you may overcome your insomnia.

When you try all sorts of strategies and still experience stress and insomnia almost daily, what should you do? It's time to see a doctor that my husband learned in a workshop on "Hypnosis" years ago. It traced back to the training program of the US military. Understandably, soldiers have to adapt to various situations and need to fall asleep fast. They must get enough rest so that they can perform tasks once they wake up. My husband has used it for many years, and it's very effective.

From a medical point of view, hypnosis is a form of psychological therapy. It's intended under professional supervision to change the state of awareness by relaxing the body to improve focus and concentration. This differs from the portrayal of hypnosis in popular culture, where the hypnotized person loses control, and his behavior is manipulated by another person. Although the second form of hypnosis has statistical data to explain its phenomena, conclusive results from scientific research are lacking.

Self-hypnosis to fall asleep is just one application using the principle of hypnosis. It relies on one's own will and imagination, leading to the desired goal of falling asleep fast.

In practice, we first lie flat on the bed, ensuring there are enough blankets after we fall asleep. Then we learn to lie still and relax the muscles of the whole body. Starting from the top of the head, we check if our face is relaxed. If we are unsure, the easiest way is to tighten our eyes and mouth, then loosen them up slowly. Afterwards, we move on to the neck and shoulder. We check on the fingers. Any tense areas need to be loosened and remain relaxed.

The second step is to imagine a machine that scans from head to toe, and you, like a bystander, trace the scanning beam. During the scan, you keep breathing slowly and deeply. Imagine that the beam is moving downward, from the forehead, eyebrows, eyes, bridge of the nose, lips... If you realize the beam has missed a part, backtrack and continue. You can always start it all over. After it passes the neck, let it do the left arm first, all the way to the tip of every finger. Let it return to the neck and do the right arm. Let it go back again and continue down the body. In such a manner, you have it scan the whole body. Whenever you are distracted, tell yourself not to think but to focus on the body. The entire body can be scanned at a normal speed in two or three minutes. Repeat the process if you are still awake. After you practice this regularly, you can fall asleep quickly.

I once did a comparison in winter. On the first night, I wanted to up after 20 minutes. The next night, I used self-hypnosis and imagine that there was a warm spring flowing through my body. Within three minutes, my body warmed up. I didn't understand why, but it worked.

Being unable to fall asleep is frustrating. Whatever method we use, we must first determine that we "need" adequate sleep for health reasons and for functioning properly the next day. Self-hypnosis cannot guarantee that you'll fall asleep. Since a lot of research has been done about this method, you should at least give it a try, which is better than tossing and turning in bed for a long time.

Chapter 7: Regular Checkups

When I reached age fifty, our insurance policy covered colonoscopy, a procedure that allows the doctor to examine the large bowel and the distal part of the small bowel by a scope with a camera.

The procedure itself isn't painful because you usually don't feel anything after the sedative injection. However, the preparation beforehand is daunting for it involves: (1) eating low-fiber foods for three days, (2) going on a clear liquid diet one day before, and (3) drinking a prescription laxative drink to clean out the bowel.

I debated whether to have it done.

Should I do it? None of my family members has a history of colon cancer.

On the other hand, the anesthesia-related risk and some discomfort shouldn't deter me from an insurance-covered procedure, right?

At last, I mustered up my courage and made an appointment.

The doctor removed a large polyp packed with cancer cells!

Unlike most people who undergo colonoscopy once every 5-10 years, I went through it three times that year since my doctor worried the cancer cells might have escaped from the polyp into surrounding areas. Fortunately, the two follow-up procedures didn't detect any sign of cancer.

My primary care physician told me, "You're a lucky lady. They caught it in the nick of time."

learned about my cholesterol and glucose problems through my annual physical, which led me to alter my diet and add exercise to my daily routine (see Chapter 3).

Besides the insurance-covered preventive care in the US, a few years ago, we took a medical trip to Taiwan. Several hospitals in Taiwan, including the famous Taipei Veterans General Hospital, offer a whole-body-MRI-for-tumor screening (GI tract not included) at NT$42,000 (equivalent to about $1,400). We paid less than $1,000 back in 2011. As a comparison, the average cost of a *localized* MRI in the US is about $1,300.

During that trip, the results turned out well for me and my husband. However, they found my cousin had early-stage prostate cancer. Even scarier, one of our friends had pancreatic cancer. Neither of them had symptoms nor felt any discomfort. After returning to the US, our friend went to his doctor right away. He had another MRI done for the pancreas, which confirmed pancreatic cancer. Then, he scheduled an appointment with an oncologist. Following the surgery, the doctor commented, "In my 20+ years as a surgeon, I've never caught pancreatic cancer at such an early stage. You must be doing something right."

After our friend told him about his medical trip to Taiwan, the doctor said, "Thank you for sharing this piece of information. I'm going to make a special trip there."

What happened to my cousin's prostate cancer? His story went equally well. He caught it so early that the doctor was able to give him proper treatment.

As of today, both of them are still cancer-free.

So, besides regular checkups in the US, if you can, you might consider taking your next vacation in Taiwan for a whole-body MRI screening. It may even save your life.

Chapter 8: Know Your Pills

The Food and Drug Administration (FDA) first allowed emergency use of the Pfizer–BioNTech vaccine on December 10, 2020, to fight against COVID-19. Yet in August 2022, the report on https://usafacts.org/ showed the following national vaccination rate: 78% of the population have received at least one dose and 66% are considered fully vaccinated.

Why do people hesitate to receive the vaccine? Numerous reasons exist. Many excellent studies and articles dealt with this subject. One of those reasons has to do with the fact that people tend to lump vaccines together with medications and resist them because of perceived risks.

I understand their concerns. I've been working in the pharmaceutical industry all my life and have interacted with the FDA for quite a few years. A new prescription drug must go through five steps:

1. Discovery/concept: For example, someone in a company comes up with an idea of developing a new drug to treat diabetes. They go ahead and synthesize novel compounds.

2. Preclinical research: Evaluate the compounds in test tubes and animal disease models to ensure their safety and effectiveness.

3. Clinical research: Select one lead compound and evaluate it in human clinical studies to confirm its safety and effectiveness. Submit

4. FDA review/approval: The FDA follows a rigorous evaluation process to determine whether a drug provides benefits that outweigh its known and potential risks for the intended population.

5. Post-market safety monitoring: Continue to track the drug's safety and effectiveness in patients.

The above information probably has already given you a subtle cue that all medicines can cause side effects. My knowledge in the field led me to develop a philosophy: Don't take medications unless necessary.

Yet, sooner or later, most of us will run into a situation in which we have no choice. My time came shortly after I reached forty. That year's annual physical checkup revealed I had high cholesterol (total cholesterol, 342; LDL, the bad cholesterol, 267; HDL, the good cholesterol, less than 10; triglycerides, 187).

My primary care physician, Dr. Stone, gave me a stern warning. "You need to diet and exercise so that you could control your total cholesterol to be <200, LDL at <100, and triglycerides at <149. Also, your HDL must be higher than 50."

Although I knew well only about 20% of the cholesterol in my bloodstream came from food and my body made the rest, I took her advice and started a stringent routine of diet and exercise.

Three months later, nothing improved, and Dr. Stone prescribed Lipitor. The most serious side effect of Lipitor is myopathy, a dysfunction of the muscle fibers. In a few weeks, I developed severe muscle aches, and my doctor put me on Vytorin.

Everything went well until I failed to get up one morning. My whole body hurt as if a high fever had hit me. Dr. Stone sent me to see a cardiologist right away because she worried the drug might have damaged my heart muscle. Luckily, a stress test revealed my heart function had not decreased.

Back to square one. Dr. Stone stared into my eyes. "I'm giving you the five-milligram Crestor, the lowest dose. If you develop side effects, I don't know what else to give you."

Again, everything seemed well. I told my husband, "Finally, something works for me."

Then, one day, my son Jon grasped my right palm, and I shrieked with pain.

Jon stared at me with concern. "Are you okay?"

I bumped into something? I didn't remember injuring it.

During the next few days, the lump grew so big that I could no longer close my hand to make a fist.

Back in Dr. Stone's office, I gazed at my hand and wondered what went wrong with my health. She examined the swelling. "I'll send you to an orthopedic surgeon right away."

Dr. Philips, the orthopedic surgeon, checked the X-ray pictures. "Looks like a badly inflamed tendon."

"How can it be? I haven't had any accidents or injuries." I scratched my forehead.

"Repetitive motions can also cause it." He surveyed the films again. "You have a few choices: physical therapy, medications, cortisone shots, or surgery."

I opted for the first.

Three weeks later, my condition became so severe that even picking up a teacup turned into a challenge. My physical therapist gave up. "It's not working at all. You need more aggressive treatment."

I returned to Dr. Philips. He examined my boxing glove-like hand with obvious sympathy in his eyes. "I'll give you an injection today. Be prepared. It'll be the worst shot you've ever had in your life. Afterward, the inflammation will subside."

He numbed the area before sticking the needle into the gap between my fingers. I gritted my teeth. Excruciating pain shot through my hand and up every nerve into my shoulder.

Within a week, the swelling on my hand went down, but I found two more bumps on my left arm. This time, I reached my conclusion—the side effect of Crestor. With Dr. Stone's permission, I stopped taking the statin for two months. My tendon problem eased. Unfortunately, my cholesterol went back to over 300. Dr. Stone warned me, "You must go back on Crestor. Although tendonitis is painful, at least it won't kill you."

Back to my research mode. I found a CardioChek Analyzer lipid profile kit on Amazon to monitor my total cholesterol, HDL, and triglyceride levels at home and conducted a one-person clinical study on myself. I found that by taking one milligram of Crestor, I could control my parameters without the problem of tendon inflammation.

Later, I shared my experience with several friends, which

recently, "I cut my Lipitor in half. Not only is my cholesterol still less than 200, I no longer feel weak and groggy every day. Thank you for alerting me about the side effect of my medication."

So, if you find your hair falling out in clumps, check whether your pills are causing it. Many common medications, such as those for high blood pressure, psoriasis, and arthritis, are linked to hair loss. And if you take pills to prevent osteoporosis, be aware that long-term bisphosphonate therapy has been linked to a type of thigh fracture called an atypical femoral fracture. Nearly half of the adult population in the US has high blood pressure. Are you one of them? If so, watch out for medications (anti-inflammatory drugs such as ibuprofen, certain antidepressants, and oral steroids) that undermine the effectiveness of your hypertension meds.

I usually read the package insert for my medications, which lists numerous potential side effects. If you don't have the training to understand it, seek help from your pharmacists or friends. Spending time and effort to learn more about your medications will do you a lot of good in the long run.

Chapter 9: Depression

As Christians, no matter what happens, we should always express joy and gratitude toward God to serve as powerful witnesses for Jesus. Right?

Devout Christians who suffer from depression may feel ashamed to tell others because they blame it on their lack of faith in God's healing power. If I prayed more, trusted God more, and read my Bible more, would the depression go away? Yet, my own experiences tell me those so-called "religious activities" seldom help. For total healing, we must acknowledge that faithful followers of Jesus Christ do fall into depression.

So far, research still hasn't pinned down the exact causes of depression. You can find information about potential factors on trustworthy websites (e.g., the Mayo Clinic website).

My depression began after my mother passed away. I've written about that part of my life in a book entitled *The Way We Forgive* (under my pen name, R. F. Whong). Below is an excerpt.

> *Many nights I lay awake. Faint noises from the hallway roused my hopes. Mom's shuffling to the bathroom. As I came back to my senses, I couldn't help but burst into tears. She'd never live with us again.*
> *Sympathetic words from others just brought more misery.*

Everything under the sun is meaningless. Please take away my life."

Yes, feelings of sadness and hopelessness accompanied me every minute. I experienced a sleep disturbance. Remorse and guilt filled my soul with questions such as, "Would Mom still be around if I'd only done..."

I couldn't function like before and had difficulty concentrating and making decisions.

Several times on the highway, I fought the temptation to swerve my car to the opposite lane. The only thing that held me back was my mother's words, "Live, and live an abundant life as our Lord Jesus has promised us."

The weird fact was that I didn't want to seek medical help.

My husband, a trained professional counselor, recognized my symptoms. Still, he couldn't make me go to my doctor and could only ask brothers and sisters from church to pray for me.

I visited the library and read many books about death and near-death experience. By God's grace, certain articles pointed me toward a potential source of my problems. After my dad passed away when I was sixteen, I didn't have the luxury of processing my grief properly because my aunt, whom I've loved since childhood, kicked my mom and me out of our shared house. The unresolved grief, along with my aunt's betrayal, injured my soul. Throughout my life, I worked hard to suppress my hurt. After becoming a Christian, I felt ashamed of my fear of death and my resentment toward my aunt. I became a control freak in vain attempts to exert power over the uncontrollable.

Since Mom's death was beyond my control, I spiraled into depression.

The final breakthrough came one morning as I kneeled before the Lord and cried out, "Did You walk with my mother when she traversed the valley of death?"

"Yes, I did." A clear message popped into my head. I shot up to my feet, goose bumps crawling all over my body.

From that day on, I gradually emerged from my cocoon of despair.

During that difficult period, my husband played a crucial role in my recovery. In addition, my own prayers and the prayers of others helped sustain me. I'm convinced the power of prayer is beyond

Everybody's situation is unique. My depression was situational, and with the support of friends and family members, my recovery was possible once I came to terms with my mother's death. With a chronic depressive disorder, although its cause isn't fully understood, disturbances in the levels of certain chemicals, such as neurotransmitters, may be the culprit. Some will need to see a doctor and take medications.

I should offer one piece of advice from my experience: You can't be alone in depression. You need to have someone by your side to support you. If you don't have family members around you, reach out to trusted individuals in your faith community.

Last but not least, be assured that God, the Almighty Healer, will walk with you through the deepest, darkest valleys.

Chapter 10: About Money

When I studied at the University of Illinois for my MBA in finance, I learned something crucial, not from my textbooks but from a professor's comment. "Making money is important, but how to manage what you have is even more critical."

Financial health depends on what you do in both areas.

All too often, we hear about big lottery winners who later lost it all.

I read this piece of news online some time ago with interest. "Five years after a Kentucky resident won a $27 million jackpot, he was penniless and living in a storage shed with his wife. The couple squandered their fortune on the typical goodies that sink so many lucky winners. They bought dozens of high-end cars, mansions, and a plane…"

In my mind, managing my money takes precedence over bringing in new money. In this booklet, I'll share my tips on the management side and also touch upon investment.

Some questions may pop up at the mention of investment.

Should Christians invest in the stock market? Is it like gambling? What does the Bible teach about investing?

Remember Jesus' parable about the three servants and their given talents? In Matthew 25:14-30, Jesus talked about a man who, before he left for a trip, summoned his three servants and entrusted them with individuals doubled their money, while the third person dug a hole in the ground and hid his talent. When the master returned, he gave the third servant a hard time.

People often ask, "What did the third servant do wrong? Wasn't it the right thing to do to keep the master's entrusted treasure safe by burying it? Why did he get reprimanded? What would the master say if the other two invested and lost their money?"

My reply below is based on my understanding of God's attributes. The master had the entire world under his sovereignty. Loss or gain wasn't his primary concern. What he wanted from the three servants was their obedience to his command to make good use of what they had. Risks and challenges are critical ingredients of the abundant life that the Lord has promised us.

Everything, including my life, is entrusted to me temporarily. My responsibility as a manager is to well use what God has given me according to His guidance.

So, I not only invest in stocks but also trade options.

In my MBA program, I learned a lot about different techniques related to financial management, yet three key principles from my professors benefitted me more than anything else.

The first principle: The US market is very efficient. When a piece of news reaches you, likely most people have already learned about it. In other words, don't believe what others tell you about which stock to buy and don't invest in anything you don't understand.

The second principle: At any given time, the pool of money is fixed. When someone loses money, where does the money go? To another person. If you want to make money, pay attention to those who constantly lose money and try to do the opposite.

The third principle: Risks and returns always go hand-in-hand. Higher returns mean greater risk. There is no such thing as a no-risk investment. Even money in your checking/saving account, seemingly safe on the surface, encounters two risks: opportunity cost (the failure to use cash in an economically efficient way) and inflation.

As shown in the following chapters, I derive most of my practical investment strategies based on these three pieces of advice.

Chapter 11: Income, Expenses, and Personal Financial Statement

I must reiterate the advice from my professor that weighs more than gold. "Making money is important, but how to manage what you have is even more critical."

The starting point to manage your current circumstance? Conduct a thorough analysis.

In finances, that means you'll have to track income and expenses, which sounds easier than it is.

I've often served as a financial planner free of charge for people in my church. Once, a brother asked me to help him. I told him, "Okay, here's an excel sheet. Please track your income and expenses for three months, then we'll discuss how to invest."

He tried it for two weeks and gave up. Without that critical piece of information, I could do nothing for him.

You may ask, "Why three months? Do I have to do it every year? It's a pain in the neck."

What is the reason for doing it for three consecutive months? The average data after three months of tracking will provide a better understanding of your financial status because sometimes monthly income and expenses are irregular. For example, we pay our estimated tax quarterly, not monthly.

No, you don't have to do it every year. From my experiences, you life that potentially affects your financial situation. For example, you move to a different city, receive an outstanding promotion, or add a child...

The table at the end of this chapter is a comprehensive list of items to track. At this point, you sigh and wonder, "Can I do it? It looks tedious and may involve a lot of work."

Remember what I discussed earlier (Chapter 3) about the "habit loop"—the trigger (or cue), the routine, and the reward?

Trust me. You can do it once you build it into a habit.

For me, I identified my journaling as the place to add this extra step into the routine. I collected all the information and receipts and simply jotted them into my diary. Then, once a week, I transferred the entries into my excel sheet, which looks exactly like the table shown at the end of this chapter, except that now I can conduct my calculation. Drop me a note on my website, and I'll email you the excel spreadsheet.

Meanwhile, put together your personal financial statement, which is a snapshot of your financial position at a specific point in time.

First step: List your assets (what you own), which include cash in CDs, checking, and saving accounts, securities such as stocks, bonds, and mutual funds, life insurance (cash surrender value), personal property (autos, jewelry, etc.), real estate (market value), and retirement funds (e.g., IRAs, 401k).

Second step: List your liabilities (what you owe), which include current debt (credit cards, loans), taxes you need to pay, real estate mortgages, etc.

Third step: Subtract liabilities from assets to get your net worth.

Like a balance sheet in a company, this should be done at least once a year.

Again, drop me a note on my website, and I'll email you an excel spreadsheet. Or, you can easily google and find a similar one.

You have taken the first step. The reward? You know your net worth and how much extra money you can pour into investment.

Ruth Wuwong

	Days			
1. Monthly Income	1	2	...	31
Salary				
Other pay				
Investment income				
Scholarships				
Money from other sources				
Total Income				
2. Monthly Expenses	1	2	...	31
Mortgage				
Gas/electricity/water				
Garbage				
Groceries				
Child education				
Medical expenses				
Car payment				
Car maintenance				
Gasoline				
Home maintenance				
Household items				
Health insurance				
Life insurance				
Car insurance				
Long-term care insurance				
Home/rental insurance				
Meal out (+ coffee/drinks)				
Clothing/shoes				
Cable TV				
Cell phone/phone				
Internet service				
Holidays/gifts				
Vacation/travel				
Entertainment				
Beauty parlors/grooming				
Religious/charitable				
Stationaries/postage				
Income tax/ property tax				
Other				
Total Expenses				
3. Monthly Cash Flow = Monthly Income – Monthly Expenses				

Chapter 12: Invest in Education

Before we invest in the stock market and other productive assets, I must emphasize that investing in education to broaden your knowledge will help you achieve your financial goal in the long run.

I mentioned previously that my husband, Ken, is a retired pastor, and I'm a biochemist by training. A few years after we got married, the amount in our combined checking account improved a bit, from less than fifty dollars to a few hundred dollars.

The pastor's pay wouldn't impress anyone, but it was decent. Working for a pharmaceutical company, I made twice as much as Ken. With our combined income, why did we still struggle to pay bills every month?

I realized both of us knew nothing about finances.

After many prayers, I sat my dear hubby down for a chat. "One of us must learn how to manage money. You or me? Take your pick."

The answer? Me.

Ken had no interest in money at all. Otherwise, he wouldn't have quit his civil engineer job to become a pastor.

In the beginning, I went to the library and read quite a few books about the stock market, bonds, mutual funds, etc. The more I studied, the more frustrated I felt. In the end, I concluded that if I wanted to do it right, I should try to get a complete education. So, I bit the bullet and entered the University of Illinois for my MBA degree in finance.

I must admit that those years were very challenging because I worked during the day and attended school at night. Even as an in-state student, the tuition fees became a burden. I had to forego a few "must-haves." We grew most of our vegetables in the summer, seldom ate out, and only bought second-hand furniture and cars. I learned to purchase my formal outfits (e.g., two-piece suits) at Goodwill and the Salvation Army.

After four years and about $20,000 out of my pocket, I completed the program. Boy, was it worth it!

I didn't change my career path and mainly used my knowledge to manage our own finances. And what a difference it made. In a short while, the combined number of our checking, saving, and brokerage accounts increased to more than $50,000.

Along the way, we not only learned to manage our money but also gained some precious insights.

First, owning things brings short-lived pleasure, but knowledge, like experience, stays with us for a lifetime.

Second, learning broadens our perspective and enriches our worldview. Getting skills related to your job or about how to manage money is outstanding. Yet obtaining new knowledge on various subjects (e.g., gardening, different cultures and cuisines, music appreciation, a new language, etc.) unrelated to your work can make your life more interesting and enhance your relationship with others.

Third, don't attempt to keep up with the Joneses. Stick to your principles and be content. As an example, I used to have a subordinate who drove a Mercedes. At one point, especially after we had acquired a sizable asset, I asked Ken, "Should we consider replacing our old Toyota Camry with a Mercedes?"

My wise hubby replied, "Why? Is it necessary? It's not just the upfront payment. The additional expenses, such as insurance, repairs, and maintenance, are all higher."

Yeah, he was right.

Chapter 13: Stocks and Options

Stocks: Buy Low, Sell High.

In an earlier chapter (Chapter 10), I talked about why the third servant in Jesus' parable who buried his entrusted treasure was reprimanded. I also shared that everything, including my life, is entrusted to me temporarily. My responsibility is to obey the Lord and make good use of the *talent* assigned to me according to God's guidance.

What is the key element embedded in this belief? Learn. Work hard.

If I try to invest in stocks but don't want to do research, it's gambling. Think about the fact: Professional investors have the tools, spend hours analyzing the market, and still can't make money all the time. As an amateur, how can I expect to win?

We all wish we can buy a stock at its lowest point and then sell it at its highest point.

But how?

Unfortunately, no one can provide a winning formula. However, methods exist for us to study a specific company to pin down a price range to get in and another (higher) price range to get out. I'm a lifetime member (one of my best investments) of the National Association of Investors Corp. (NAIC) and have benefited from their stock selection guide.

Interested in learning more about how to estimate future growth rates and predict a stock's potential return? You may want to check out the NAIC's website at www.betterinvesting.org.

Sell Put Options to Buy Stocks.

You have done your research and identify a few stocks you like. The only problem? According to your analysis, the stock's price is currently not in the *buy* range.

Many of you already know that you can use a limit order to buy or sell a stock at a specific price. For example, if you want to spend $90 per share to purchase shares of a $100 stock, you can set a limit order that won't be filled unless your specified price becomes available.

There is another way to do it. You can sell a put option.

What is a put option? It's a contract that gives the option buyer the right to sell a particular stock to you (the option seller) at a predetermined price known as the strike price, within a specified window of time. To induce you to sign the contract, the buyer will pay you an option fee, the premium, right now (i.e., the moment you sell the put).

The following is a real case study from my records.

For some time, I wanted to own a certain stock, but its price was always outside the buy range of my analysis. When the stock's price was $33, I sold five put options at a strike price of $31, with a target time of one month (i.e., the contract would expire after a month). For your information, one option is 100 shares. In another word, I entered a contract with the option buyer that he/she could force me to buy the stock at $31 one month later if the stock price fell below $31. The premium wasn't much, only $0.8/share. So, I pocketed $400 from the five puts ($0.8*500 shares = $400).

One month later, its stock price was $34. The option expired, and I didn't get to buy the stock. I still desired the stock and sold another five put options at a strike price of $33, with a target time of two months. Because this time the contract was for two months, the premium was higher at $1.6/share. I pocketed $800 ($1.6*500 shares = $800). When the option expired, I still didn't get to own the stock and sold another four rounds of put options.

The market crashed in March 2020 because of COVID-19, and that stock's price fell to $23. I was forced to buy 500 shares at $31 premium of $8.5 per share, my actual cost to buy the stock was $22.5 ($31 minus $8.5) per share. A few months following the March 2020 market crash, the price of this stock returned to $34. By the way, this stock pays a good dividend (~$1.8 per share at ~4%), much better than the bank.

To sum up, if you have done your research and really want to own a certain stock, but its price is outside your buy range, then sell puts. If its price doesn't fall, you get to keep the premium money. If the whole market crashes because of certain disasters (e.g., COVID-19), and you're forced to purchase the stock, you'll likely own it at a discounted price.

Sell Call Options to Sell Stocks.

Although I highly recommend using the "sell-puts-to-buy-stocks" strategy, I must caution you about selling a call option to sell a stock.

Like a put option, a call option is a contract that gives the option buyer the right to buy a particular stock from you (the option seller) at a predetermined price known as the strike price, within a specified window of time. To induce you to sign the contract, the buyer will pay you an option fee, the premium, right now (i.e., the moment you sell the call).

I mentioned above that I was forced to buy a stock at $31 when its price fell to $23 in March 2020 because of COVID-19. After selling six rounds of put options with a cumulated premium of $8.5 per share, my actual cost to buy the stock is $22.5 per share, and this stock pays a decent dividend. Recently, the stock traded at around $36.

Should I sell? What do you think?

My answer is: It depends.

As an investor, generally I try to own my stocks for as long as possible, especially if the stock pays a good dividend. Under certain circumstances, however, I may need to rebalance my portfolio and will consider selling a stock.

For example, I used to work for a pharmaceutical company and received a lot of stocks as a portion of my compensation. Suddenly, I realized 50% of my entire portfolio was on that stock. Therefore, I had to diversify to reduce my exposure to risks. Let's assume that the stock price was $120. Instead of selling that stock outright, I sold five options at a strike price of $120 with a target time of one month. The

$122 per share. I was forced to sell 500 shares at $120. However, I actually sold it for $123.4 per share.

It sounded good. The problem? That year, the capital gain put me into another tax bracket.

I would emphasize again that everything, including my life, is entrusted to me temporarily. My responsibility is to obey and be a good steward according to God's guidance. After paying a hefty tax bill that year, the Holy Spirit reminded me that owing a lot of tax because of poor planning wasn't a good use of the assets that God has entrusted me. Later, I found a better way to rebalance my portfolio: Donate the stocks to my church or nonprofit organizations of my choice.

To some of you who don't usually itemize but give regularly, please consider setting up a donor-derived charitable fund and make a large sum of donations, and you'll receive a tax deduction in the current year. You can then donate out of that fund over time in the next few years.

Additional Notes on Execution.

First, to trade options, you'll need to open a brokerage margin account. With a margin account, you can borrow money to invest in stocks. But please don't borrow any money for your investment. Only invest in the stock market when you have extra, dispensable cash.

Second, I mentioned my professors' comments in an early chapter (Chapter 10) and would like to reiterate it: The US market is very efficient. When a piece of news reaches you, likely most people have already learned about it. Thus, don't believe what others tell you about which stock or option to trade. Do your research and draw your own conclusion. You can read and study what others have to say about your chosen stock/option of interest. Yet take those opinions with a grain of salt.

Third, remember my MBA professor's other advice? At any given time, the pool of money is fixed. When one person loses money, it goes to someone else. If you want to make money, figure out who constantly loses money and do the opposite.

Trading option is trickier than stocks because of the time element. As you buy a stock, you own a piece of that company, and your ownership won't expire until you decide to sell. Options are different because it's not ownership but a contract. When the time is up, the option becomes useless.

Many online sites advertise you can achieve a weekly return of 5% by trading options (mainly from buying them). Yet, according to the stock platform Etoro, 80% of day traders lose money over the course of a year with a median loss of 36.3%. The Wall Street and other sources estimate that 90% of investors lose money buying options.

It's a fact that most people who buy options lose the premium at the expiration of the contract. To make money, do the opposite and sell options.

Fourthly, don't be tempted to sell naked options (i.e., selling a call option without owning the shares, or selling a put option without cash to fulfill the obligation at the option's expiration). It's against the principle of balancing risks and returns.

Even though different option trading strategies (e.g., butterfly spread, straddle…) look alluring, I stick to my approach and use options as a tool to buy and sell stocks. Thus, for put options, I set aside cash in preparation to purchase the stock of interest should its price fall below the strike price in my sold option. And I only sell covered calls (i.e., selling call options on the stocks I own).

I remember one time I shared my tips with someone at church, and a month later, he reported back to me. "Your strategy doesn't work. I was forced to borrow money to buy 1000 shares of XXX stock."

I replied, "I've never borrowed money to buy stocks."

The same individual later made another mistake. "I followed your strategy and sold three contracts of puts to buy ZZZ stocks. Guess what? I'm now stuck with 300 worthless shares."

I challenged him. "Did you research ZZZ and concluded you truly wanted to own a piece of the company for the long run?"

He scratched his head. "A friend told me ZZZ just discovered a big gold mine in Africa. I thought it was a good bet."

Well, don't bet. Do your analysis and be a trustworthy steward of whatever God has entrusted to you.

Chapter 14: Asset Allocation and Real Estate

Don't put all your eggs in one basket.

We've all heard this proverb. What's the philosophy behind it? Minimize the risk of losing all you have.

Asset allocation aims to balance risk and reward by placing your hard-earned eggs into different baskets. No simple formula exists for every individual because each of us has different goals, risk tolerance, and investment horizons. For me, I'm willing to take risks for higher returns as long as the investments don't disturb my sleep at night, and I still have peace of mind day in and day out.

The three main asset classes—equities, fixed-income, and cash and equivalents—have different levels of risk and return. In general, the higher the risk, the better the return.

If you need $20,000 for a new car next year, you probably shouldn't put the money into the stock market. Even though the bank interest rate is low, at least by the time you need money for the purchase, you'll have it.

This simple example illustrates the key point: Analyze your current and future situation carefully and put together the investment strategy accordingly.

Of course, nobody can predict the future. The interest rate may go up or down, and stocks will fluctuate. When the interest rate rises, the attractiveness of growth equities decreases. Difficult to win, right?

Ultimately, human lives are in God's hands. Our responsibility is to project and manage.

Numerous books and online articles provide excellent advice about asset allocation: setting aside cash for emergencies, the 60/40 (60% equities/40% bonds) formula, etc. So, I won't delve into the details of those practices. Instead, I'll share how I allocated money to real estate after the collapse of the housing market in 2008.

Buy low and sell high.

We attempt that goal for stocks and other investments as well. But how does one know something has hit its bottom price?

There is no sure way to catch the lowest point. Yet, when the market spirals downward, and everybody is getting out, it's a clear sign to take action.

I watched the burst of the housing bubble with great interest. In late 2009, I checked our bank's interest rate and told Ken, "This is our once-in-a-lifetime opportunity. I think we can have a better return by putting money into real estate."

During a business trip to San Francisco, I checked Zillow.com and noticed a bank-owned house in the East Bay listed for $260,000. A few years ago, the house had sold for $580,000.

I called a broker friend, and we toured the house in the evening. Within a month, we took out a home equity loan against our primary residence and purchased the place.

Back in Chicago, we found a bank-owned condo listed for $140,000. I asked our broker to make a cash offer of $94,000, and the bank accepted it.

In 2010 alone, we bought four rental properties.

For sure, being a landlord is hard work, and it's not for everyone. We hired property managers to maintain the rental properties for us. The reward was that the annual return, after expenses, was better than the bank interest rate. Furthermore, once the housing market stabilized, all the houses appreciated substantially.

That East Bay house in California? Since its value increased so much, we donated it to a Charitable Remainder Trust (see Chapter 16 for more information) to manage our tax liability.

Maybe another bubble of some sort will happen soon and provide an opportunity for one more serious asset allocation.

Chapter 15: Entrepreneurship

Do you ever dream of becoming your own boss so that you can plan your schedule and earn a decent income?

An article by Dragomir Simovic published on July 28, 2022, shows the following statistics:

* Ninety percent of new American billionaires are self-made.
* In 2016, 25 million Americans were starting or already running their businesses.
* The number one reason businesses fail? Lack of a market need for the product.
* Forty-six percent of small business entrepreneurs are between the ages of 41 and 56.
* There are 582 million entrepreneurs in the world.
* Twenty percent of small businesses fail within the first year.

Studies show middle-aged men start the most successful businesses.

Type "entrepreneurship" in the Amazon search box and over 60,000 books will pop up. Rather than replicate those books, I would like to share my experiences.

Stage 1: Planning

The idea of starting my own biotech enterprise came to me when my former employer canceled my project and moved me to a different department. I'd invested a few years of my life in developing new truly believed our effort would eventually help many patients. Then, my company got out of the kidney disease drug sector.

Since I'd taken part in extensive marketing research conducted by the giant pharmaceutical firm where I used to work, I understood the market and competition. I also kept myself well informed about the cost, risks, and challenges of developing a new drug (see Chapter 8 for the five steps involved in bringing a new prescription drug to patients).

I let my idea sit for two years. After many prayers, I put together a business plan and resigned from my job.

Stage 2: Launch

The first step, an easy one, was to incorporate my company.

The much more difficult next step was to secure funding. Back then, we had intangible assets such as ideas, know-how, and experience. But we didn't have patents or anything tangible to attract investors. Through my professional connections, I found several angel investors (wealthy private investors who finance small business ventures in exchange for equity) who shared my ideology. With a $600,000 fund, we set up a lab to start preclinical research.

Stage 3: Move Forward and Maintain

Anyone who has ever worked in the biotech sector will appreciate the fact about how fast research burns cash. We pinched pennies. Still, the initial fund evaporated in less than a year. Fortunately, our first few compounds all tested positive. With the data, we applied for the NIH SBIR (National Institutes of Health Small Business Innovation Research) grants.

To make a long story short, we received six NIH grants and raised two more rounds of funds from investors. The money allowed us to bring our compounds into clinical studies.

Stage 4: Exit

Ten years later, some of our original investors grew restless. When would they see a return on their investment?

We had outstanding data from a clinical study on ten hemodialysis patients. The next step required about $20 million to evaluate the compound in 200 more patients. Would we manage to find the money?

After numerous discussions, our board reached a decision and sold the program to a venture capital firm. Instead of raking in over $200 million with data from a Phase II clinical study, we sold it for about ten times less with the existing data.

Our original investors were well pleased because they received more than a ten-fold return.

The example from my own story is to warn you that, if you are interested in becoming an entrepreneur, please research the four stages described above carefully before you quit your job.

You must estimate the net difference in your income between the current job vs. your new endeavor. In my case, my biotech venture paid me options instead of cash until we received the NIH grants. I prepared for it during the planning process, and our family lived on my husband's income and our investment earnings for a few years.

Another important part of the planning is to analyze the breakeven point of the operations in your new business. Don't be overly optimistic about your potential gain and underestimate the costs and risks. Since it's notoriously difficult to conduct this analysis in the biotech industry, I told all our investors that there was a >95% chance that their money would go down the drain.

Last but not least, never start a business with zero or little experience in the relevant industry. For an entrepreneur, both training and know-how are absolutely crucial. Without my technical background and years of experiences in developing new drugs, my small company would not have attracted the interest of angel investors.

Chapter 16: Retirement and Estate Planning

Nowadays, the term "aging gracefully" seems popular among baby boomers. It could mean "showing signs of growing old, but still moving forward." To me, instead of lamenting about entering the Medicare age, I consider it God's blessing that I still hang around. Many of my friends didn't get the luxury of growing old.

One of my husband's popular seminars is entitled "Love them once more," a tongue-in-cheek presentation on how to manage the last leg of your life so you don't impose unnecessary burdens on your loved ones. The following are some key points.

Purpose in Retirement.

If you type "retirement" in the Amazon search box, you'll find over 70,000 results. How to keep your savings on track, when to collect social security, and what to do for health care… From *Retirement Planning Guide* to *1001 Fun Things to Do in Retirement*, you can take your pick from numerous excellent books.

I won't reinvent the wheel here, but rather share our personal experiences.

We all look forward to the day when we don't have to report to the office and can travel year-round.

And, for us, that day finally arrived.

For the first time in a long while, my husband, Ken, didn't have to brought excitement. A long weekend? What are you talking about? All weekends were too long for him.

His calendar contained no commitments, but also no structure.

After two extended vacations, boredom set in. He needed something to do.

No, we can't travel nonstop like the gentleman we met on our last cruise who spent 26 weeks on the same ship. It would drive us nuts.

Should Ken sign up for more volunteer work? He didn't want to find random activities to kill time. He needed purpose and direction—a new assignment from the Lord so that he could continue to serve in His kingdom.

One of our friends took early retirement and became a missionary in a foreign country.

That was a possibility, but there were many more.

After some seeking, Ken discovered what the Lord wanted him to do.

Yet, everyone is distinct in his or her own way. The key is to pray about it and let the Holy Spirit guide you into your personalized new adventure.

Powers of Attorney (POA), Long-term Care Insurance, and Revocable Living Trust.

If I am fortunate enough, I may reach an age in which my brain no longer functions well. I'll need another person to make major decisions for me. That's when a POA comes into play.

A POA is a legal document that allows another person to make financial or medical decisions for us. In general, we'll need two POAs, one for finances and the other for healthcare. There are some nuances about POAs. You can easily find more information through an online search.

Should I purchase a long-term care insurance policy? Is it worth it? According to the Administration for Community Living, a 65-year-old person has a 70% chance of needing some type of long-term care in the near future. In 2021, the median annual cost of a home health aide was $61,776, and that of a private room in a nursing home was $108,405. If you are super-rich or very poor, don't worry about it. However, for most of us, buying a policy is a wise decision. Like medical insurance policies, you should do it while you're still healthy

If you start early, you pay premiums over a longer period, but the rate is cheaper and locked in for life.

What about setting up a revocable living trust?

Revocable living trusts, as the name indicates, can be changed over time. They're useful to avoid probate, minimize estate taxes, and protect the privacy of you and your beneficiaries. However, the drawback is that you must hire an attorney to draw up the document and you also need to monitor it on an annual basis and make adjustments as needed. Moreover, you must designate beneficiaries on your retirement accounts and establish transfer-on-death provisions for all non-retirement accounts.

The aforementioned paragraphs aren't meant to give you all the information you need but to prompt you to conduct more research on the subjects.

Charitable Remainder Trusts (CRTs).

I mentioned in a previous chapter (Chapter 14) that I picked up a rental property in the San Francisco East Bay when the housing bubble burst. After my husband retired, we decided to sell that house to retrench our investment in real estate.

There was one serious problem. That house's value increased so much that, if we sold it outright, the tax liability was unbearable.

During that period, we prayed about it on a daily basis. By chance, I happened upon an article about Charitable Remainder Trust (CRT), which I wasn't familiar with. After more research, we considered it as God's answer to our prayer regarding the East Bay house.

What is a CRT? Here is the definition from Wikipedia:

"A Charitable Remainder Annuity Trust (CRAT) is a Planned Giving vehicle that entails a donor placing a major gift of cash or property into a trust. The trust then pays a fixed amount of income each year to the donor or the donor's specified beneficiary. When the donor dies, the remainder of the trust is transferred to the charity. Charitable trusts such as a CRAT require a trustee. Sometimes the charity is named as trustee, other times it is a third party, such as an attorney, a bank, or a financial advisor."

However, the information on Wikipedia isn't 100% accurate. In our case, we set up a CRT for 20 years, which means that the remainder of the trust is transferred to our chosen charity at the end of die during the CRT duration? Then it automatically goes into our revocable living trust (see above). Moreover, instead of naming someone as a trustee, my husband and I serve as the trustees for our CRT.

Please note that a CRT is irrevocable and complex. You must involve a good lawyer to have it done right. Through the charitable organization we chose, we got in touch with an outstanding Christian attorney who guided us through the entire process.

More About Estate Planning.

The following paragraph is from a friend of ours, Ronald Tolleru, who serves as the Director of Planned Giving and Special Gifts at Trinity International University.

"The primary objective of estate planning is to ensure that your wealth or stuff reaches the persons and organizations you intend for it to reach, at the time and in the form you desire. The secondary objective is to plan the transfer to minimize taxes and other expenses."

Yet, a majority of Americans do not think about estate planning. After a lifetime of working and accumulating an estate, in the end, most people leave the decision of how to depose their properties after death to the state law.

As I emphasized again and again in previous chapters, we, as Christians, should consider everything entrusted to us as temporary. Estate planning is an important step in our effort to be good managers for God and to invest in eternity.

So, as we age, we do what we need to do. Set worries aside and look heavenward.

Chapter 17: Conclusion

One million—1,000,000—symbolizes your life.

With the number **One** intact, all the opportunities become available and achievable.

Remember: Our health is the number **One** that is followed by many zeros. Without that **One**, all those zeros amount to nothing.

I mentioned previously that health, wealth, and relationships intertwine, and it is difficult to single any of them out. As a Christian entrepreneur, to decipher the intimate links between health, finances, and relationships has been my lifelong quest.

One area that I haven't addressed in this booklet is relationships. I left it out on purpose, for it requires an entire book on its own.

My husband and I fit the theory of "opposites attract." He is a night owl, and I'm an early bird. He, a type B personality with a relaxed, patient, and easy-going nature, does not become stressed when he fails to reach his objectives. I, on the other hand, a typical type A, strive toward my goals with a constant sense of urgency at an expense of a balanced life.

During our 40+ years of a wonderful marriage, how did God work in us so that we not only get along well but also help each other achieve equilibrium in body, money, and marriage?

With the Lord's mercy, I hope to share more of my life with you in my next booklet. Meanwhile, I would love to hear your story and note anytime at the "Leave Comments" page of my website (www.ruthforchrist.com). I welcome guest writers as well.

***

Action Plan: Develop Your Action Plan. An example is shown below. Use the same format for your other action plans to improve your health and finances.

Purpose: To form a habit of exercise every day
Goal: Achieve a visible/measurable change in six months
Evaluation Process: Check weekly to see if your new habit sticks.
Evidence of Success: After six months, check to see if you've made a visible/measurable change in your goal (e.g., exercise every day, lose weight…)
Results/Accomplishments:

Timeline	Things to Do	Support
Step 1 (Week 1):	Write what you want your health to look like.	Go over your list with someone you trust.
Step 2 (Week 2):	Examine your daily routines and identify one "habit loop"—the cue, the routine, and the reward.	Review Chapter 3.
Step 3 (Week 3):	Add an easy-to-do exercise (e.g., ten sit-ups) to your routine without changing the cue and reward.	Share your newly modified routine with your trusted friend.
Step 4 (Weeks 4-7):	Keep up the good work.	Share your progress with your friend at least once a week.
Step 5 (Week 8):	Add another easy-to-do exercise to your routine (e.g., stretching for three minutes).	Share your newly modified routine with your trusted friend.
Week 9 and onward:	Repeat Steps 1-5 until you achieve your goal.	Enjoy the new you.

A Note from the Author

Thanks for reading. If you like the book and have a moment to spare, the author would appreciate a brief review. Thank you for your help.

Check out the author's fiction books under her pen name, R. F. Whong.

Love at the Garden Tomb: Love—one plus one can't be two.

The Way we Forgive: Love, forgive, and live.

About the Author

Wuwong spent twenty-one years as a scientist and then as a marketing manager for a global pharmaceutical company. About twelve years ago, she and her friends founded a biotech company (www.vidasym.com) with a focus on developing new drugs targeting chronic kidney disease. As the company's president, chief scientific officer, and chief financial officer, she successfully raised more than 20 million dollars for Vidasym from angel investors, the National Institutes of Health, venture capital firms, and pharmaceutical companies.

Wuwong has published 120+ scientific papers and books (using her legal name, J. R. Wuwong) plus a few non-scientific books/articles (using her pen name, R. F. Whong). Currently, she lives in the Midwest with her husband, a retired pastor. They served at three churches from 1987 to 2020. Their grown son works in a nearby city. As a pastor's wife, she often provided free financial planning advice to congregants. In the spirit of servanthood, she also volunteered as a tax preparer in the AARP Foundation Tax-Aide program during the past eleven years.

To connect with her, please go to www.ruthforchrist.com

Part II:
The Chinese Version
第二部分：
中文版

健康和財務

一名基督徒企業家的探索

路得

Ruth Wuwong, Ph.D., MBA

免責聲明

本書中的資訊僅用於教育和娛樂目的。 作者已盡全力提供準確、可靠、完整的資訊。 並不提供法律、財務、醫療或專業建議。且無聲明或暗示任何保證。

對於本書中的資訊直接或間接造成的損害或金錢損失，作者均不承擔任何法律責任。

ISBN: 979-8-88904-004-0

Published by Vidasym Publishing
A Division of Vidasym, Inc.
5013 S. Louis Ave., #532
Sioux Falls, SD 57108

健康和財務

内容 Content

路得

致謝

首先，我將此書獻給我的救主，主耶穌基督。

此外，我謹將本書獻給多年來支持我們事工的主內弟兄姐妹。

書評

自 12/2022 發行以來，九个月內本書已獲得 42 則 Amazon 好評。以下是最近的一則書評。

Top reviews from the United States

 Nancy N.

★★★★★ **Two books in one!**
Reviewed in the United States on September 19, 2023
Verified Purchase

這是我所讀該作者的第二本書； 我喜歡她的寫作風格，因為非常實用。 我認為這本書是兩本書合而為一的，我真的很喜歡。第一部分是關於如何保持和改善健康，第二部分是關於金錢。正如作者所說：「賺錢固然重要，但如何管理你所擁有的更關鍵。」我最喜歡的一章是關於股票和資產配置的那一章。 我喜歡作者以易於理解的方式解釋這些概念，讀完這一章後我意識到購買股票並不像我想的那麼複雜，而是我實際上可以做到的。 我向所有想要改善健康和財務狀況的人強烈推薦這本書。」

健康和財務

第一章：簡介

早些時候，我們見到了四十多年未見的莉莉。當年我在俄亥俄州立大學讀研究所時，莉莉把我當她自己妹妹一樣照顧。我告訴丈夫健，「莉莉已經八十多歲了，身體不好。我們應該專程去看她。」

　　拜訪一位老朋友，勾起了許多回憶，有些痛苦，有些甜蜜。在我們一起閒聊時，莉莉問道：「記得你父親在你十六歲的時候就去世了。你媽媽曾經對我提起過，你有不好的遺傳傾向，包括高膽固醇、糖尿病、和體重問題。我注意到你媽媽超重並且患有糖尿病。你在這裏讀書時，即使才二十歲出頭，也顯得有些胖。現在看看你。已經六十多歲了，對吧？你苗條而健壯。這些年來你都做了些什麼來克服那些先天的障礙？應該分享你的經驗。相信其他人會從中受益。」

　　她的話引發我產生如此強烈的情緒，以至於變得有些結巴。回憶在我腦海中洶湧澎湃，無法終止。

　　上帝引導我們度過了難以克服的挑戰，才達到目前的狀態——不僅是健康，還有財富和良好的人際關係。

路得

不同的教會事奉，也曾為不少夫婦做過輔導。我发现一個有趣的現象。糟糕的人際關係影響幸福指數，也阻礙人們逐夢。我們可能知道金钱上焦慮對人際關係有負面影響。反之亦然。疾病也會破壞婚姻和妨礙個人追求經濟獨立。事實上，健康、金錢、和人際關係如此緊密地交織在一起，以至於很難將其中任何一項單獨列出來討論。

當然，我們不像比爾蓋茨或沃倫巴菲特那樣富有，但已經沒有財務上的煩惱。結婚時我們兩人支票賬戶中總額不到五十美元。然而，一路走來，經過很長的一段路，我們 2007 到 2021 年的納稅申報表上，即使只是投資方面的收入（利息、股息、和資本收益），每年平均超過 200,000 美元。我們可以按照自己的需求提早退休，也能向選定的非營利組織捐贈大筆資金。

我這樣的經驗會對一些人有幫助嗎？

因著我的教育背景（正道神學院基督教研究碩士，俄亥俄州立大學生物化學博士，以及伊利諾伊大學財政和管理碩士），一向我寫的文章學術意味偏重，一般人常说不好理解。這本小書是我第一次嘗試用外行人的語言來談我對管理錢財及健康方面的技巧和策略。

希望我的分享對你有助益。

健康和財務

第二章：您的身體，您的健康

1,000,000。

假若您的健康是數字一，後面跟著許多零（每個零代表您所珍惜的東西之一）。沒有那個一，所有的零都算不上什麼。

大家都知道健康很重要。許多人花大把金錢和精力來維持健康：避免吸煙/吸毒、減少攝入酒精、改善飲食、鍛鍊、每晚有充足的睡眠…… 清單確实很長。

有人可能會問：「如何定義健康？我沒有任何病。算不算健康？」

其实這是個有趣的問題。

儘管因目的不一樣，「健康」的定義或有些許差異，但根據世界衛生組織（WHO）的說法，健康是「身體、心靈、和社會關係上完全健康的狀態，而不僅僅是沒有病和虛弱。」世衛進一步澄清：「健康是一個積極的概念，強調社會和個人資源，以及身體的能力。」

美國疾病控制與預防中心（CDC）的數據顯示，2017 年美國的醫療保健費用為 3.5 兆美元，但美国人預期壽命低於其他已發展國家。

路得

　為什麼？

　找不到簡單的答案，也不是本文的重點。

　確實，雖然當提到健康這詞時，身體健康會自動浮現在腦海中，但精神、人際關係、和財務健康同樣重要。許多研究表明，這些生活中的不同層面彼此相互交織，深刻地影響一個人的總體健康形態。

　例如，人際關係好的人有較佳的能力來處理困難和痛苦，因而得著更好的情緒健康。 心靈健康的人較能感受平靜和建立人生的目標，促使他們在其他方面努力，實現更好的生活。

　回到身體健康這話題，沒有捷徑。要想有好的身体，一定要在飲食、運動、和睡眠中建立起好的習慣。

　这本書有大半是講说我如何为健康問題想出解決方案的分享。希望對您有幫助。

第三章：習慣的養成

大多數人每天都會刷牙。 我們是如何養成這習慣的？ 很可能是，在了解到刷牙對於保持口腔衛生的重要性之前，父母就幫助我們養成刷牙的習慣。

　　大家都知道飲食和運動對於改善身體健康至關重要。 然而，為什麼許多人無法養成每天有正確飲食和鍛鍊的習慣？ 為什麼不能像刷牙一樣簡單？

　　四十出頭的時候，每年一次的體檢顯示我的膽固醇高得驚人，而且糖化血紅蛋白（HbA1c，衡量過去兩到三個月的平均血糖水平的指標）呈高趨勢。

　　醫生建議我改變飲食習慣並減輕體重。

　　如果不做改變，高膽固醇和糖尿病的綜合遺傳很快就會搞砸我的健康。 我父親早逝，不知道他有沒有高血脂。 但是我所有的叔叔姑姑都遭受了高膽固醇導致的不良後果，例如中風或心臟病。 在我母親那邊，外祖父和我一个舅舅死于肥胖和糖尿病相關的併發症。 我媽媽也超重和患糖尿病。 最終，她死於糖尿病引起的中風。

　　然而，我可以做什麼來改變我的飲食習慣並開始鍛练呢？

究來處理問題。 試著多了解飲食和運動的资訊後，我發現一些有趣的事情：大多數人失敗，是因為沒有意識到要有正確飲食和持續運動的唯一方法就是將它們變成習慣。 例如，一旦你養成了鍛练的習慣，就像早上刷牙一樣，比較有可能堅持下去。

因此，我進一步研究如何養成習慣這個課題。

有些人可能聽說過如何在 21 天形成習慣的公式。 然而，據倫敦大學學院健康心理學研究員 Phillippa Lally 博士宣稱，一個新習慣可能需要兩個多月才能成形，而要成為每天必做的習慣則需要八個多月。

難怪要養成天天鍛练的習慣如此困难。

查爾斯・杜希格（Charles Duhigg）在他的《習慣的力量》一書中將習慣的形成歸因於一種稱為「習慣循環」的心理模式——觸發器（或提示）、例行程序、和獎勵。

研究顯示，養成新習慣的一個有效方法是保持你的提示和獎勵，而稍微改變例行程序。

根據個人經驗，我非常支持這種做法。

首先，我剖析了自己的日常生活。

多年來，我一直遵循 No-B-No-B（不讀聖經-不吃早餐）的每日靈修習慣。 以下是我的「習慣循環」。

提示：鬧鐘在早上 6 點響起。

例行程序：起床，刷牙，洗臉，然後讀聖經禱告做晨更。

獎勵：精神平靜，準備開始新的一天。 此外，現在我可以享受早餐了。

怎麼做能修改我的例行程序，却維持相同的提示和獎勵呢？

請注意以下提示：不要試圖一下子改變你的整个程序。 相反地，試著加入一些小步驟，將小而易實現的活動插入到例行程序中。 否則，注定要失敗。

經過考慮，我在禱告後加了十個簡單的仰臥起坐。

健康和財務

糟糕，沒我想的那麼容易！

在我急着想吃早餐而后衝出門去上班的情況下，我得強迫自己去完成那看似簡單的運動。　隨著時間的過去，新的小變動終於堅持下來。接著，我又增加了伸展運動，甚至足部按摩。　事实上，例程只加多了十分鐘。　我已經這樣做了 20 多年，真正受益於每天的晨練。

然而，我自知每天需要三十分鐘的鍛鍊，最好包括有助心血管的運動。

回到原點重新来過吧。

我觀察到另一個「習慣循環」：下班後，接兒子放學回家，然後洗了個澡，好像是要洗去一天工作所帶來的焦慮和煩惱。

下面乃是與這習慣相關的「提示-例行程序-獎勵」。

提示：我回到家，把手提包放在沙發上。

例行程序：洗澡。

獎勵：我感到神清氣爽，準備好做晚飯了。

可以在洗澡前運動嗎？　為什麼不行？

跟着，我從小處著手。　通過廣泛的在線搜索後，我得出結論，跳繩應該是个好選擇，因为不需要花什麼錢及用太多空間。　此外，跳繩提供許多好處。　除了是有效的有氧運動外，還可以增強平衡感和敏捷性，並提高骨質密度。

第一天，我跳了十下，已經氣喘吁吁了，好像剛跑完馬拉鬆一樣。　也難怪，從中學起就沒跳過繩。　我當場決定砍半，每天只跳五下。　從那個微小的開始，事情慢慢好起來。　儘管如此，我還是花了整整一年的時間才增加到跳三百下。　後來我把三百下分成 5 環節，每節跳六十下，中間加入柔軟体操和舉重。

從各方面來說，我的例行程序只增加了 20 分鐘，卻獲得了巨大的好處。　不僅將體重指數（BMI）控制在標準範圍內，我感覺更強壯、更有活力。值得一提的是，過去二十年裡我的

路得

BMI 指數一直保持不變。

說完運動，那飲食方面呢？可是完全不同的考量。

我喜好美食，曾試過節食但無濟於事。 當肚子餓的時候，能拿到手的任何食物，我都会塞入嘴裡。 在反思飲食習慣後，我決定少量多餐。 換句話說，不惜一切代價避免進入渴食的狀態。

我發現除了三餐外，我的日常生活還包括兩次喝咖啡的休息時間，一次在上午 10 點左右，另一次在下午 3 點。

以下是與該習慣相關的「提示-例行程序-獎勵」循環。

提示：我看了看手錶。 上午 10 點，該喝咖啡休息了。

例行程序：我起身，喝杯咖啡，然後随手拿一塊当天公司提供的任何甜品。

獎勵：我感到放鬆、滿足，準備好重返工作崗位。

是否有可能带些健康食品在休息期間享用呢？

因此，我保持了相同的提示/獎勵，而用蘋果或香蕉代替了甜品。 漸漸地，我養成了現在一天吃六餐的習慣。

早餐（早上 7 點）：低碳水化合物，例如二分之一杯乾酪，或一個中等大小的鱷梨，或一杯由蔬菜和水果製成的冰沙。

上午小吃（10 點左右）：水果或酸奶。

午餐（中午時分）：碳水化合物，如麵條或意大利面，外加一個雞蛋和蔬菜。

午後小吃（下午 3 點左右）：水果或酸奶。

晚餐（下午 6 點時分）：避免碳水化合物，只吃肉和蔬菜。

夜宵（晚上 9 點左右）：水果。

通過少量多餐，我得以避免血糖和胰島素水平飆升的模式。我母親在四十多歲時患上了糖尿病。 截至今天（已近七十鍊、和足部按摩都幫助了延遲糖尿病發。

對飲食的另一個提醒：避免加工食品。 如果可能的話，盡量用新鮮食材從頭開始，這樣更健康也更經濟。

如上所述，我早餐經常吃乾酪 (cottage cheese)，但並不好吃，幾乎沒有味道。 為了讓它更開胃，過去我常加入果醬，雖然店里買回來的果醬含有高比例的添加糖。

好不好用自製的醬料代替商店裡的果醬？

幾年前一個夏末，花園裡的櫻桃番茄藤上留下了數百個未成熟的果實。

扔掉它們嗎？ 太浪費了。

經過一些研究，我將它們打成泥狀，然後加入糖和麥芽糖（增稠）煮沸。 最終產品是 自製的綠色醬汁，非常適合我的干酪。 因為加了一點糖，沒有防腐劑，所以我把它們冷凍在小袋子裡，每週解凍一袋。 如果你有興趣收到食譜，請告知，我樂意分享。

到目前為止，我只談到良好的習慣。 如果您有吸煙、吸毒、或酗酒等不良習慣怎麼辦？ 能否通過「提示-例行程序-獎勵」循環來改掉不健康的習慣？

也許可以。 但有些問題需要專家介入，不在這文章的範圍內。

如果可能的話，我建議您加入一個問責小組。

有好幾個月，我參加教會的一個問責小組。 四個女的，每週見一次面。

最初，我們專注於報告過去一周所做的事情，包括是否每天閱讀聖經、鍛鍊、和保持飲食健康。 分享幫助我們認識到自己的壞習慣，也互相鼓勵養成好習慣。

小組很快就超越了健康問題。當彼此的信任度提升後，我們分享了工作、配偶、孩子等各方面的問題。其中一位姐妹當時面臨著一個兩難的境地；是否攻讀神學博士學位。 在問責小組的幫助下，她做出了決定。 幾週前，她發了一條信息给我，感謝我当年給她的鼓勵，告訴我她現在是舊約神學博士，並經常在各種活動中發表演講。

希望我的分享能讓你看到，養成正確飲食和每天鍛鍊的習慣是可行的。 也許你還會因此獲得神學博士學位呢。

健康和財務

第四章：反射療法--足部按摩的好處

受過西方生化科技博士學位的熏陶，我曾經反對任何與中醫和替代療法有關的事情，但一次上海之行改變了我的信念。

在香港探親期間，我們決定繞道中國大陸。那時，中國剛對遊客開放。旅行團一抵上海，我的一顆牙齒出了問題，疼痛分分鐘變得難以忍受。令人驚訝的是，酒店裡有一個牌子，上面寫著一位專門從事足部反射療法的醫生進駐在那裡。

「我得試一試。」我低聲對丈夫說，臉因痛苦而扭曲。「無論如何，死馬当活馬醫吧。」

我走進醫生的辦公室，看到一位壯碩的中年婦女獨自坐著。她疑惑地望了我一眼，但沒有說話。

「我——我——」我操着普通話，苦笑著皺起眉頭，覺得自己很傻。

「有什麼事嗎？」她的語氣輕柔，和体態不成比例。

我嚥了嚥口水。「我來這裡是看牙痛。」

她示意我坐下。「請脫掉你的鞋襪。」

我按照她的吩咐做了。她用酒精徹底擦拭了我的右腳，然後近得过支氣管炎？」

我吃驚地張大嘴巴。她怎麼知道的？

她轉到我的另一隻腳。過了一會兒，又瞄了我一眼。「你的家族有糖尿病背景。」

我再也控制不住自己的好奇心了。「你能從按我的腳看出來我的病史？」

「当然。」她給了句簡單的回答，又回去工作了。「哪顆牙給你添麻煩？」

我張開嘴，指指罪魁禍首。

她點點頭。「做好準備。我會用力按壓你的一個腳趾。非常疼，但你的牙痛會消退。」

疑惑湧上心頭，我並不完全相信。接著她按住我右腳的第二個腳趾，我痛到差點從椅子上跳起來。

「牙齒感覺如何？」她的語氣平靜而親切。

淚水在我的眼里打轉。不知道是否腳趾太疼分散了我的注意力，牙痛竟消失了。「有用。」

「嗯。但是疼痛會回來的。下次開始的時候，就按摩這個穴位。」她指給我看腳趾上的確切位置。

她又指了指我腳底的一小塊區域。「對了，按這裡可以延緩糖尿病的發作。」

我帶著迷茫的心情走出了她的辦公室。一進酒店房間，我忍不住脫口而出：「老公，你不會相信發生了什麼事。」

聽了我的描述後，他搖搖頭。「我不信。簡直像變魔術。」

我交叉雙臂。「你為什麼不自己去看看？」

「但我沒病呀。」他撓了撓頭。「你說只花了二十塊人民幣嗎？連五美元都不到。好，我這就去。」

按了我的腳，说我以前得過闌尾炎。還問我為什麼要見她，因為我的健康狀況很好。」

令人驚奇，不是嗎？

一個簡單的谷歌搜索會得到大約 485,000,000 個有關足療的結果。 您可以花幾塊錢輕鬆地購買一個簡單的足部按摩工具。雖然有很多書詳細說明了在哪裡按摩最有效，我發現最直接的方法是按摩你的整個腳，包括底部、腳背、和腳趾。 不要弄得太複雜，否則你遲早會放棄。 保持簡單，讓按腳成為一種每天的習慣。

自從遇到那位了不起的足療醫生以來，每天早上我都按摩腳。 我母親在四十多歲時患上了糖尿病。我早就過了那個年齡，還沒有发病。也許足部按摩確實可以延緩糖尿病的發作。

路得

第五章：維生素 D

您读過這篇題為「維生素 D 如何影響 Omicron 症狀」的文章嗎？ 如果有興趣读该文，請在我的網站 www.ruthforchrist.com 上留言，我會發給你。

這是那篇文章裏的一段：

「低維生素 D 水平可能和嚴重疾病相關，包括 COVID-19。但如果要有增強免疫的好處，必需是標準的低劑量而不是大劑量。」斯皮爾曼博士加以说明。

大約 20 年前，我開始在維生素 D 領域進行研究。了解到每天攝入 400 IU 的維生素 D 是不夠的。所以，我自動增加到每天 1000 IU。

當醫生說我缺乏維生素 D 時，想像一下我的震驚。我沒有任何症狀，除了有時關節會痛，而且很容易患輕度感冒。她給了我一張 50,000 IU 超大劑量的處方。我從她手中接過紙張，但沒有去拿藥。為什麼？因為我知道，服用維生素 D 過量導致 高鈣血症的副作用會對我的身體有害。我自已將每日攝入量提高到 2000 IU。非常有效。我的維生素 D 水平恢復正常，並且關節不再疼痛，也少了經常性輕度感冒的困擾。

維生素 D 是維生素嗎？

健康和財務

大多數人會回答：「當然。」

然而，正確的答案可能會讓您大吃一驚。

許多人都知道，暴露在陽光下，皮膚會生產維生素 D 。但那是沒有活性的。它需要在肝臟和腎臟中進行化學變化以形成活性代謝物骨化三醇。

像雌激素或雄激素一樣，骨化三醇是一種激素，必需與核受體結合。一旦它與維生素 D 受體（VDR）結合，就會激活 VDR 以募集眾多輔助因子來形成轉錄複合物，以調節 200 多個靶基因。

眾所周知，維生素 D 對骨骼健康至關重要。 其他證據表明，VDR 在調節心血管、免疫、代謝、和其他功能方面發揮著重要作用。 例如，來自流行病學、臨床前、和臨床研究的數據表明，維生素 D 缺乏將增加心血管疾病風險。因此，維生素 D 的好處不僅僅在於構建和維持強健的骨骼和牙齒。

為了改善您的整體健康狀況，請記得每天服用 2000 國際單位的維生素 D3。

路得

第六章：壓力和睡眠

壓力會對身心造成嚴重破壞，影響您的睡眠、飲食，甚至是日常的鍛煉。生活中的一些特殊情況，例如搬到新地方、換工作等，往往會導致壓力劇增。然而，如果只是平淡日子，如何在日常生活中意識到有壓力的存在呢？

幾年前，我在一家大型製藥公司擔任項目經理。在我沒有意識到的情況下，工作量一點一點地增加。很快地，我連夜裡都在想工作的事，竟然患上失眠。

如果您曾經有過不眠之夜，就會知道那是多可怕的事。身體需要休息，但腦袋不想合作。我像大海中的波濤般輾轉翻騰。無論怎麼努力，都無法入睡。然後早上又來了，我還得拖著睡眠不足的身體去上班。

根據美國睡眠醫學學會的數據，大約三分之一的美國人患有周期性失眠症。當您有一個多月的睡眠困擾時，就會形成一種慢性病。我們十個人中有一個可能就患有這種慢性疾病並需要治療。

健康和財務

許多因素（衰老、咖啡因、疼痛、藥物、呼吸暫停、壓力⋯⋯）都會導致失眠。眾所周知，壓力會影響睡眠。另一方面，失眠也會導致有壓力。這是一個惡性循環。

在思考一翻，確定了壓力是我一個多月以來難以入睡的原因後，我問了幾個人，「我該怎麼辦？」

「辭職吧。」教會一位女士打趣道。

抱歉，实在沒有辦法不工作。

另一個基督徒狠狠地看了我一眼。「信心多一點。禱告，把一切交給主。」

一位朋友建議：「晚上喝一杯酒。會讓你昏昏欲睡。」

我做了一個在線搜索，了解到酒精可能會讓您一開始感到困倦。但是隨著酒精的代謝，它會干擾睡眠。一項研究表明，男性喝兩杯，女性喝一杯，會降低 24% 的睡眠質量。

應該向醫生索取安眠藥嗎？在製藥行業工作了一輩子，我形成了一種理念：除非絕對必要，否則不要服用藥物（相關信息請參見第八章）。

一天早上靈修的時候，我再次把我的問題帶到主面前，一個想法突然出現在我的腦海裡。「培養一個可以讓你用手而不是大腦的嗜好。」

是的，這正是我所需要的。

在研究了不同的手工之後，我決定學做珠寶，主要是因為它不需要很大的空間。我去了一所社區大學上課，每天晚上九點以後，就把公司的事放到一邊，專心用雙手做事。令人驚訝的

路得

失眠症。

　　除了培養愛好之外，運動、靜思默想、按摩等都有帮助。嘗試使用積極的方式來管理壓力。從長遠來看，看電視或上網等被動的方式都有可能使壓力增加。

　　當您嘗試了各種方法卻仍然幾乎每天都經歷焦慮症時，該怎麼辦？是時候去看醫生了。

　　關於如何養成好的睡眠習慣，您可以通過谷歌搜索「睡眠習慣」找到許多有益的文章，這裏不需重覆。若遵循我在第三章中所討論的「提示-例行程序-獎勵」的方法來形成新的習慣，相信您一定可以改善睡眠。

　　最后，分享一个自我催眠入睡的方法。這是美國軍方訓練軍人，如何在 2 分鐘之內入睡。軍人因要適應各種環境，爭取睡眠，以便隨時醒來就可以執行任務，的確要學會倒頭便睡。

　　这方法我的另一半多年前在一次《催眠》(hypnosis)的講座中学会，已經採用多年，非常有效。

　　催眠，從醫學的角度看，是一種生理和心理的治療方法，目的是在專業督導下，改變對環境的覺察，幫助身體放鬆，改進專注能力。這與流行文化中，被催眠的人完全失控，由外人操縱行為的情況有所不同。後者雖然有統計數據來解釋現象，但在科學研究的領域，還沒有一致的定論。

　　自我催眠入睡，狹義的解釋與應用，是如何靠自己意志和思維，盡快入眠，獲取足夠休息。

　　進行的時候，首先是平臥在床上，先確定入睡後有足夠的保暖衣被，然後不再翻來覆去，學習全身肌肉放鬆。先從頭頂開始，自我省察，臉上肌肉是否放鬆？若不確定，最窄易是先把

健康和財務

眼睛眉頭嘴巴等繃緊，然後慢慢放鬆。之後注意脖子肩膀是否放鬆，手指有否握拳等等。任何明顯有肌肉收緊的部位都要先放鬆，已經放鬆的部位要繼续保持。

第二步，是想像有一個機器，從頭到腳掃描一次，而自己在旁追踪橫切的光線。專注掃描的時候，要保持緩慢深呼吸。想像光線慢慢的經過身體，例如頭頂、前額、眉毛、眼睛、鼻樑、鼻子、嘴唇等，若發現忽略了一個部位，可以退回那裡繼續，甚至從新掃描。到了脖子後，就要先做左手，一直到每一根手指。回到脖子，轉向右手，一直到指尖。再回到脖子，繼續身軀往下。如此有次序的，把全身掃描一遍。一旦分心，要自我提醒深呼吸，放鬆，不要想其他，專注身體。在正常的速度下，兩三分鐘可以全身走一遍。若仍然清醒，可以再來一遍。經常訓練，一趟下去，很快就可以放鬆睡著。

我在冬天的時候，曾經做了一次比較。一天晚上，嘗試讓自己身體感到疲累而睡著，躲進被窩 20 分鐘後，手腳才開始暖和。第二天，採用自我催眠法，「想像」有一道暖流通過全身，專注放鬆，不到三分鐘，身體就暖和起來。我不懂為什麼，反正有效。

身體疲倦想睡卻睡不著，是一件令人苦惱的事。無論用什麼方法，必須先確定，為著健康和翌日事務，我們「需要」睡覺。自我催眠不能保證一定入睡，但既然經過許多研究試驗，不妨試試看，總比在床上輾轉反側良久不能入睡好受。

路得

第七章：定期体檢

五十歲時，醫療保險涵蓋腸道檢查（醫生用照相機鏡頭查看大腸內部）。

過程本身並不痛苦，因為在全身麻醉後通常不會有任何感覺。但是，事先的準備工作令人望而生畏，因為包括：（1）吃低纖維食物三天，（2）前一天吃清澈流質食品，（3）喝處方瀉藥清潔腸道.

我掙扎著要不要做。没必要做吧？我的家人都沒有結腸癌病史。另一方面，麻醉相關的風險和一些不適，不應該就讓我放弃保險給的福利，對吧？

終於，我鼓起勇氣，預約了。

醫生切除了一個充滿癌細胞的大息肉！

大多數人每 五到十 年接受一次腸道檢查，我在那一年就做了 三次，因為醫生擔心癌細胞可能已經漫延到其他區域。幸運的是，這兩個後續程序沒有發現任何癌症跡象。

我的家庭醫生告訴我，「你真幸運。他們在關鍵時刻鏟除癌症病変.」

健康和財務

此外，也是通過定期檢查時我知道了膽固醇和初期糖尿的問題，讓我改變了飲食習慣，並在日常生活中加強鍛鍊。

這是為什麼我認為每個人都需要定期檢查。

除了美國的保險所包的檢查外，我得分享一下我們幾年前去台灣的一次醫檢旅行的經驗。台灣的幾家醫院，包括著名的台北榮民總醫院，都提供全身核磁共振（MRI）進行腫瘤篩查（不包括胃腸道），費用為新台幣 42,000 元（約合 1,400 美元）。我們在 2011 年支付的費用不到 1,000 美元。相比之下，在美國光是局部 MRI 的平均費用約為 1,300 美元。

在那次醫檢旅行中，我和丈夫都一切正常。然而，他們發現我表弟患有早期前列腺癌。更可怕的是，我們的一位朋友患有胰腺癌。他們倆都沒有症狀也沒感到任何不適。回到美國後，朋友立即去看醫生。又做了一次胰腺核磁共振檢查，證實他患有胰腺癌。接著，他安排了見腫瘤科醫生。手術後，醫生對他說：「在我 20 多年的外科手術生涯中，我從來沒有切除過這麼早發現的胰腺癌。你一定是做對了些什麼。」

在朋友告訴他台灣醫檢之旅後，醫生說：「謝謝你這條信息。我也要去那裡做一次特別的旅行。」

關於我表弟的前列腺癌，也同樣順利解決。由于發現得早，醫生能夠給他適當的治療。

直到今天，他們倆都沒有癌症復發。

所以，除了在美國做定期檢查外，如果可以的話，你應該考慮下次去台灣度假，做全身核磁共振檢查。

也許一次旅行可以挽救你的生命。

路得

第八章：認識您的藥丸

美國食品藥品監督管理局（FDA）於 2020 年 12 月 10 日首次允許緊急使用輝瑞疫苗來對抗非典肺炎。然而 2022 年 8 月的報告（https://usafacts.org/）顯示國家接種率如下：78% 的人口至少打了一劑，66% 的人打了全部疫苗。

為什麼不是每个人都立即打疫苗？大眾對接種疫苗有疑慮存在著許多原因。不少好文章都討論過這课題，如果有興趣，您可以在網上找到。對一些人來說，可能是因擔心風險而拒絕接種疫苗，就像他們不想吃藥一樣。

我理解他們的擔憂。 我一生都在製藥行業工作，與 FDA 打交道也有好幾年。 一種新的處方藥必須經過五個步驟：

1. 發現/概念：例如，一家公司有个人想出了開發一種治療糖尿病新藥的方法。开始合成新化合物。

2. 臨床前研究：在試管和動物疾病模型中評估新化合物，来確保其安全性和有效性。

3. 臨床研究：選出新化合物中最好的一个（先導化合物），在人體臨床研究中對其進行評估，以確認其安全性和有效性。將結果提交給 FDA。

4. FDA 審查/批准： FDA 遵循嚴格的評估流程來確定藥物對預期人群的益處是否超過其已知和潛在的風險。

5. 上市後安全性監測：持續跟蹤藥物在患者中的安全性和有效性。

從上面的陳述中，您可能已經發現了一個微妙的線索，那就是幾乎每種藥都有副作用。多年的知識和經驗使我形成了一種理念：除非必要，否則不要服藥。

然而，大多數人遲早會遇到別無選擇的情況。四十歲之後不久，我的時間就到了。那一年的體檢顯示我有高膽固醇的毛病：總膽固醇，342；低密度脂蛋白，即壞膽固醇，267；高密度脂蛋白，亦稱好膽固醇，低於 10；甘油三酯，187。

我的醫生斯通立刻送我去見營養師並警告我說：「你需要節食和鍛煉，這樣才能將總膽固醇控制在 200 以下，低密度脂蛋白 100 以下，甘油三酯低於 149。此外，好膽固醇必得大于 50。」

雖然我很清楚血液中只有約 20% 的膽固醇來自食物，其餘的是身體製造的，但我還是聽從了她的建議，開始了嚴格的飲食和運動程序。

三個月後，沒有任何改善，斯通醫生為我開了立普妥。那藥最嚴重的副作用是一種肌纖維功能障礙。幾週後，我出現極度肌肉酸痛的現象，醫生改讓我服用維妥力。

一切都很順利，直到有一天早上我起不來，整個身體像發高燒一樣疼痛。斯通醫生立即讓我去看心臟病專家，因為擔心藥物可能損害我的心肌。幸運的是，壓力測試顯示我的心臟功能沒有下降。

回到斯通的办公室，她看住我的眼睛。「我現在給你最低劑量 5 毫克的冠脂妥。再出現副作用，我不知道還能做什麼。」

這一次，一切似乎都很美好。我告訴老公：「終於有一樣東西對我有用。」

接著有一天，兒子握住我的右手掌時，我痛地尖叫起來

路得

喬恩關切地看住我。「您還好嗎？」

我檢查無名指下方的區域，有一腫塊。

我撞到什麼了嗎？

接下來的幾天裡，腫脹愈變愈大，以至於我無法合掌。

回到斯通的辦公室，我低頭看著自己的手，心想我的健康到底出了什麼問題。她檢查了一下後說：「我馬上送你去看骨科醫生。」

骨科醫生檢查了 X 光照片。「看起來像一條嚴重發炎的肌腱。」

「怎麼會這樣？我沒有發生任何事故或受傷。」我搔了搔額頭。

「重複動作也能引發这情況。」他又看了片子。「你有幾個選擇，物理治療、藥物治療、可的松注射、或手術。」

我選擇了第一項。

三週後，病情變得如此嚴重，以至於拿起茶杯都成了挑戰。我的物理治療師放棄了。「根本没用。你需要更積極的治療。」

回到了骨科醫生那裡，他檢查了我的拳擊手套一樣的手，眼中帶著明顯的同情。「今天我給你打一針。做好準備。這將是你一生中最糟糕的一針。但炎症會消退。」

在將針插入我手指之間的縫隙之前，他先做了局部麻醉。但我仍咬牙切齒，劇烈的疼痛從手上傳來，傳到肩膀上的每一根神經。

一周之內，我手上的腫消退了，但我發現左臂上又多了兩個腫塊。這一次，我得出了結論——冠脂妥的副作用。在斯通的許可下，我停止服用他汀類藥物兩個月。肌腱問題得到緩解，不幸的是，我的膽固醇又回到了三百多。醫生又警告我：「你必須回去服用冠脂妥。腱鞘炎雖然很痛，但至少不會要你的命。」

健康和財務

　　發揮了做新藥研發的精神，我在亞馬遜上找到了一個血脂檢測試劑盒 （CardioChek Analyzer），在家中監測我的膽固醇，開始在自己身上做起人體實驗來了。我發現服用 1 毫克冠脂妥，就可以控制膽固醇而沒有肌腱發炎的問題。

　　後來，我與幾位朋友分享了經驗，他們也重新審查服用的藥片。其中一位最近告訴我：「我把立普妥切成兩半。不僅膽固醇仍然小於 200，我不再每天感到虛弱和昏昏沉沉。感謝您提醒我藥物的副作用。」

　　如果您發現頭髮成簇脫落，請檢查您的藥丸。許多常見的藥物，例如治療高血壓、牛皮癬、和關節炎的藥，都與脫髮有關。或若您服用藥物來預防骨質疏鬆症，請注意長期雙膦酸鹽治療會引發一種非典型的大腿骨折。

　　我通常會閱讀藥物的包裝說明書，其中列出了許多潛在的副作用。假如您沒有受過訓練不能理解，千萬請您的藥劑師或朋友幫忙。從長遠來看，花時間和精力來了解更多關於您的藥丸的信息，會帶來很多好處。

路得

第九章：我得了抑鬱症

作為基督徒，無論發生什麼事，我們都應該充滿喜樂和感恩，為耶穌做有力的見證。是不是呢？

虔誠的基督徒若得了抑鬱症，也許会認為是自己對上帝的醫治能力缺乏信心而導至疾病，因此羞于尋醫或告訴別人。如果我禱告多些，多信靠神，多讀聖經，抑鬱症會消失嗎？然而，我的親身經歷告訴我，那些基督徒常有的「宗教活動」不一定能解決問題。為了完全康復，我們必須承認耶穌基督的忠實追隨者也會陷入抑鬱的症状。

到目前為止，科學研究還沒有確定抑鬱症的確切原因。您可以在可信賴的網站上找到潛在因素的资訊（例如，Mayo Clinic，網址為 https://www.mayoclinic.org/diseases-conditions/depression/symptoms-causes/syc-20356007）。

我的抑鬱症是在我母親去世後開始的。在《原諒的方式》一書中（https://www.amazon.com/dp/B0BQ5LNLNB），我寫到了生命中的那一時期。下面是一段摘錄。

多個晚上我睡不著時，走廊里傳來的微弱聲音喚起了我心中的希望。媽媽拖著腳步去洗手間嗎？當我回過神來，忍不住淚流滿面。我至爱的

健康和財務

別人的同情之言，讓我的心更加痛苦。像先
知以利亞一樣，我懇求上帝：「夠了。陽光下的
一切都是沒有意義的。請拿走我的生命吧！」

是的，悲傷和絕望的感覺每分鐘都伴隨著我。在無眠之夜，悔恨和內疚的想法，像是「如果我那樣做了，媽媽今天還會在我身邊嗎？」抓住了我的思維。

我無法像以前正常工作，難以集中注意力和做重大決定。

有幾次，在高速公路上，我有將車轉向對面車道的誘惑。唯一讓我止步的是母親的話，「照著我們的主耶穌所應許的，活出豐盛的生命。」

奇怪的事實是，我不想尋求醫療幫助。我的另一半是一位訓練有素的專業輔導，他認出了我的症狀。但卻無法逼我去看醫生，只能請教會的弟兄姊妹為我禱告。

我去了圖書館，閱讀了許多關於死亡和瀕死體驗的書籍。靠著上帝的恩典，一些文章指出了我問題的可能根源。大約三十年前，當我父親突然去世時，因為我從小就深愛的姑姑把我和媽媽趕出了我們共同居住的房子，我沒有機會和時間處理悲傷的情緒。硬被壓下的悲痛，加上姑姑的背叛，讓我的靈魂受到嚴重傷害。一生之中，我一直在努力壓抑心中的傷痛和怨恨。成為基督徒後，我為自己對死亡的恐懼和沒能原諒姑姑感到羞愧。漸漸地，我變成了一個控制狂，甚至試圖控制不在掌控之下的事物。

我母親的死超出了我所能控制範圍，加上以往硬壓下的傷痛冒了出來，我得了抑鬱症。

醫治开始于一天早上，我跪在主面前喊道：「我母親行過死陰幽谷的時候，祢和她同行嗎？」

「是的，我與她同行。」一個清晰的信息突然出現在我的腦海中。我猛地站起身來，雞皮疙瘩爬滿了全身。

從那天起，我逐漸擺脫了絕望的繭。

路得

　　當我回想起那些時日，另一半的默默陪伴在我的康復中發揮了至關重要的作用。此外，我自己和其他人的禱告也很有幫助。我深信祈禱的力量超出了人類的理解範圍。

　　在此我得加上一句，每個人的情況都是獨一無二的。有些人可能需要看醫生和服藥才会痊愈。但有一点至關緊要的信息：您不能孤獨一個人陷入抑鬱中。您需要有人在身邊陪伴。如果您沒有家人在旁边，請聯繫教會求助。

　　请记住，您可以放心：上帝，全能的醫治者，將與您一起走過最陰深、最黑暗的幽谷。

第十章：金錢這課題

在伊利諾伊大學攻讀金融管理（ MBA ）學位時，學到了一些重要的東西，不是從書本，而是從一位教授的言談中：「賺錢固然重要，但如何管理好已有的資產更為關鍵。」

有没有健康的財務狀況取決於您在這兩方面--賺錢及管理--是否做了該做的事。

我們經常聽到彩票大贏家後來傾家盪產的故事。

前段時間我在網上饒有興致地看了這則新聞。「一位肯塔基州居民贏得了 2700 萬美元的頭獎五年後，竟身無分文，和妻子住在一间儲藏室裡。這對夫婦將錢揮霍在讓許多幸運的獲獎者淪喪的典型好東西上面， 他們買了幾十輛高檔汽車、豪宅、和飛機……」

在我看來，管理已有的錢比賺入新錢可能更重要些。 管理和投资賺錢同样需要技巧和策略。

提到投資可能有人立即會提出問題。基督徒應該投資股市嗎？ 這是不是賭博？ 聖經對投資有什麼教導嗎？

還記得耶穌關於僕人如何运用所賜才能的比喻嗎？ 在馬太福音 25:14-30 中，耶穌談到一個人去旅行之前，召集了三名僕人搞投資，錢翻了一倍，而第三個僕人在地上挖了個洞，把自己的那份藏了起來。 主人回來後，狠狠地罵了第三个僕人一頓。

常有人問：「第三个僕人做錯了什麼？ 把主人的寶物埋起來，好好保管，不是應該的嗎？ 他為什麼被訓斥？ 萬一另外兩人投資賠了錢，老闆会怎麼說？」

我的回答是基於對神屬性的理解。 主人擁有整個世界的主權， 得失不是他最關心的問題。 他對三名下人的要求，是要他们聽從他的吩咐，好好運用被託管的東西。 風險和挑戰是主應許給我們豐盛生命的重要組成因素。因為怕風險和挑战而裹足不前，本身就是失敗。

我的一切，包括生命，都是上帝暫時託付給我的。 作為管家（經理）的責任就是按照神的帶領好好加以運用。

所以，我不僅投資股市，還做期權交易。

在金融管理課程中，我學到了很多與財務相關的技巧，但教授的三個關鍵原則讓我受益匪淺。

第一條原則：美國市場效率極高。 當一則消息傳到您那里時，可能大多數人都已經知道了。 換句話說，不要相信別人告訴您要買那個股票，也不要投資任何您不了解的東西。

第二個原則：在任何既定時間內，資金總數是固定的。 當有人賠錢時，錢去了哪裡？ 去了另一個人那里。 如果你想賺錢，要注意那些是不斷虧錢的人，而後反其道而行之。

第三個原則：風險和回報總是相伴而行。 较高的回報意味著較大的風險。 沒有無風險投資這回事。 即使您的支票/儲蓄賬戶中的錢，表面上看似安全，也會遇到兩種風險：機會成本（未能以經濟有效的方式使用現金）和通貨膨脹。

我的大部分管理和投資策略都是基於這三條原則得出的。

第十一章：收入、支出、和個人財務報表

首先必須重申我的財政学教授那比黃金更寶贵的建議：「賺錢很重要，但如何管理你所擁有的更是重要。」

　　管理您目前情況的起始點是什麼呢？　就是進行徹底的分析。在財務方面，這意味著您必須知曉自己的每一单收入和支出。没錯，聽起來容易，做起来有点難度。

　　我經常為教會的兄姐提供免費財務規劃。　有一次，一位弟兄請我幫忙。　我告訴他：「這裏是一張 Excel 表格。　請仔细記錄你三個月的收入和支出，然後我們再討論如何投資。」

　　他嘗試了兩週後就放棄了。　因為沒有這條關鍵信息，我也就無法為他做任何事。

　　您可能會問：「為什麼是三個月？　我每年都必須這樣做嗎？豈不是太麻煩？」

　　連續三個月這樣做的原因是什麼？　記錄三個月的平均數據有助於更好地了解您的財務狀況，因為有時每月的收入和支出是不規律的。　例如，我們按季度而不是每月繳納预估稅款。

　　您不必每年都這樣做。　根據我的經驗，只有當生活發生可能影響您的財務狀況的重大變化時，才應該做此操作。　例如，您

路得

　　從網上您可以下載一份收支項目的完整列表（或查看本文末尾的表格）。　看了表格，您可能會嘆口氣，心想：「我能做到嗎？　看起來很乏味，很煩人。」

　　還記得我之前討論過的關於「習慣循環」的心理模式——觸發器（或提示）、例行程序、和獎勵嗎？

　　相信我。　一旦你養成了習慣，就可以輕易完成任務。

　　對我來說，寫日記是在日常生活中添加這個額外步驟的好地方。　每天收集了所有信息和收據，我將它們簡單地記入我的日記中。　然後，每週一次將這些條目轉移到我的 Excel 工作表中。　如果您想要我的 excel，請在我的網站上留言，我會把 Excel 表格用電子郵件發送給您。

　　另外一件要做的事，是匯總您的個人財務報表，這是在某特定時間點您的財務狀況的速描。

　　第一步：列出您擁有的資產，包括現金（CD 定存、支票、和儲蓄賬戶）、股票、債券、和共同基金等、人壽保險（現金退保價值）、個人財產（汽車、珠寶等）、房地產（市場價值）、和退休基金（例如 IRA、401k）。

　　第二步：列出您所欠的一切，其中包括當前債務（信用卡、貸款）、你需要繳納的稅款、房地產抵押貸款等。

　　第三步：從資產中減去債款，得到你的淨資產。

　　就像公司的資產負債表一樣，這事至少每年做一次。

　　如果您需要我的表格，請在我的網站上留言，我會把我用的 Excel 表格經電子郵件發送給您。　或者，您可以用谷歌搜索找到類似格式。

　　恭喜您，邁出了理財第一步。　獎勵呢？現在 您終於知道自己的淨資產以及有多少額外資金來進行投資了。

健康和財務

	月份和日期			
1. 每月收入	1	2	...	31
薪水				
其他報酬				
投資收益				
獎學金				
其他來源的錢				
總收入				
2. 每月支出	1	2 ...		31
房貸				
煤氣/電/水				
垃圾				
雜貨				
兒童教育				
醫療費				
汽車支付				
汽車保養				
汽油				
上門維修				
家居用品				
健康保險				
人壽保險				
汽車保險				
長期護理保險				
房屋/租賃保險				
外出就餐（+咖啡/飲料）				
服裝/鞋子				
有線電視				
手機/電話				
互聯網服務				
假期/禮物				
旅行				
娛樂				
美容院/美容				
宗教/慈善捐款				
文具/郵資				
所得稅/財產稅				
其他				
總支出				
3. 每月現金流量=每月收入-每月支出				

第十二章：投資于教育

在討論投資股票和其他賺錢方法之前，我得強調，投資教育來增強您的知識，長遠來看對您實現財政目標有極大幫助。

我之前提到過，我的另一半健是位退休的牧師，而我是生物化學博士。 結婚幾年後，我們共有的銀行存款賬戶裡的金額略有進步，從不到五十美元增加到幾百美元。

牧師的薪水不會令人發大財，但也不差。我在一家製藥公司上班，薪水是健的兩倍。 我們的總收入不算低，為什麼每個月仍然有困難支付賬單？我意識到我倆都對財務管理一無所知。經過多次禱告後，我和親愛的另一半坐下來討論。「我們中得有一個人要學會如何理財。 你或我？ 隨你挑吧。」

答案？ 是我。健對錢一點興趣都沒有。 否則，他也不會辭去土木工程師的好職位去當牧師。

一開始，我去圖書館看了很多關於股票市場、債券、共同基金等方面的書，越讀越覺得沮喪。 最後，我得出結論，如果想好好做，就應該接受完整的教育。 所以，我硬著頭皮進入了伊利諾州立大學攻讀金融管理碩士學位。我得承認，那些年非常不容易，因為我白天工作，晚上上學。 即使是本州學生，學費也成了負擔。 我們不得不放棄一些「必需品」。 大部分蔬菜

健康和財務

都是夏天種的，很少出去吃飯，只買二手傢具和汽車。 我也學會了在 舊货店購買上班用的套裝。

四年後，我自掏腰包花了約兩万美元，完成了金融学位。 不是蓋的，絕對物超所值！

我沒有轉換職場跑道，只是用新学的知識來管理我們的財務。結果大不相同。 才不到幾年，我們的儲蓄和投资的總數增加到五萬多美元。

在這過程中，我們不僅學會了如何理財，還獲得了一些寶貴的经验。

首先，花钱買東西可以帶來短暫的快樂，但投资于知識和經驗，所得的却伴隨我們一生。

第二，學習開闊了我們的視野，豐富了我們的世界觀。 取得與你的工作相關或關於如何理財的技能非常有幫助。 然而，学習與工作無關的各種新知識（例如，園藝、不同文化和美食、音樂欣賞、新語言等）可以讓你的生活更加有趣，並增進你與他人的交往。

第三，不要試圖和他人攀比。 堅持自己的原則而知足常乐。舉個例子，我以前有一個開奔馳的下屬。 有一次，在賺進一筆可觀的資產後，我問健，「我們是否應該賣掉老舊的豐田然后買部奔馳？」

我大有智慧的另一半回答說：「為什麼？ 有必要嗎？ 不僅僅是買車的付款，随之而来的保險、維修、和保養等額外費用都得考慮。」

是的，他是對的。

路得

第十三章：股票，期貨

股票：買低。賣高。

以前我談到了為什麼耶穌比喻中那個將一千兩銀子埋在地裡的仆人受到譴責。我也分享說，一切，包括我的生命，都只是神暫時托付給我管理的。我的責任就是按照神的指引善用它們。

這種信念的關鍵因素是什麼？努力做功課。盡力而為。

如果我嘗試投資股票但不想做研究，那我就沒有盡力。其實，這不是投資，而是賭博。想想這個事實：專業投資者擁有所有工具，並花費無數時間分析市場，但仍然無法每次都賺錢。作為一個業余投資者，你怎麼能指望常常贏呢？

我們都希望可以在最低點買入股票，然后在最高點賣出。但是可以做得到嗎？不幸的是，沒有人可以提供一個必勝的公式。倒是有很多方法可以分析發行股票的公司，嘗試估計買入的價格范圍和賣出的（更高）價格范圍。我是 NAIC 的終身會員（我這輩子最好的投資之一），從他們的選股指南中受益良多。

如果您有興趣了解如何估計未來增長率、預測股票的潛在回報等的更多信息，您可以去 NAIC 網站 www.betterinvesting.org 上查看。

賣看跌期權/賣權（PUT option）來買入股票.

假設您做了研究也找到了一些喜歡的股票。可是有個問題，根據您的分析，目前股價不在買入的價格范圍內。

許多人已經知道可以使用限價單以特定價格買賣股票。例如，如果您想以 90 美元的價格購買 現值 100 美元的股票，您可以設置一個限價單，沒有到指定的價格，限價單不會有效。

還有另一種方法（我認為是更好的方法）可以買入股票，那就是賣出一個看跌期權 （PUT option）。

什麼是看跌期權（賣權）？乃是一種合同，賦予期權（合同）買方在指定時間內（合同到期前）以預定價格（稱為行使價）出售給您 （期權合同賣方）某股票的權利。為了誘使您簽訂合同，買方將支付期權費（溢價）給您。

例如，有一段時間我想擁有某股票，但它的價格總是在我分析的買入范圍之外。當股票價格為 33 美元時，我開始以 31 美元的預定價格賣出 1 個月的看跌期權（即合約將在一個月後到期）。溢價並不多，僅為 0.8 美元/股。順便說一句，一份合約是 100 股。我賣出了 5 份合約，賺了 400 美元（0.8*500 = 400）。

一個月后，股價為 34 美元。合同到期了，股票沒買成。我仍然想擁有那個股票， 所以以 33 美元的價格賣出了另一個為期兩個月的看跌期權。這次因為合同為期兩個月，溢價較高，為 1.6 美元/股，我賣出了 5 份合約，賺了 800 美元。但我仍然沒有買成，后來又賣出了另外四輪賣權。

由於非典肺關，市場在 2020 年 3 月崩盤，該股票的價格跌至 23 美元。我被迫以 31 美元的價格購買了 500 股。然而，因為我已經賣出 六輪賣權，累計溢價為 8.5 美元/股，我購買股票的實際成本為每股 22.5（31 - 8.5）美元。到 2020 年 6

月，該股票的價格回到了 27 美元。過去的一個月裡，該股的交易價格約為 44 美元。順便說一句，這隻股票的股息很高（1.8 美元/股，約 4%），比銀行好得多。

總結一下這個策略，如果您做了研究並且真的想擁有一隻股票，但它的價格在您的買入范圍之外，那麼賣出看跌期權。如果股票繼續上漲，您就可以保留溢價資金。如果整個市場由於某些災難（例如 非典肺炎而崩盤，您被迫購買股票，也可能會以折扣價買成。

賣看漲期權（CALL）來賣出股票

上一周我討論了如何出售看跌期權 （PUT） 來購買股票。用該策略在您的目標價格範圍內買入股票是個好方法，在此我必須先說明，不要輕易使用看漲期權（CALL)來賣出股票。

首先，我得解釋一下什麼是看漲期權。它是一種合同，賦予期權（合同）買方行使權，在指定時間內以某預定價格（稱為行使價）向您（期權合同賣方）購買某特定股票。為了誘使您簽訂合同，買方將付您期權費（溢價）。

上一周我提到了由於非典肺炎，某股票在 2020 年 3 月股價跌至 23 美元時，我被迫以 31 美元的價格買入五百股。因我已賣出 6 輪 PUTs，累積了 每股8.5 美元的溢價，我購買股票的實際成本為每股 22.5 美元。在過去的一段時間裡，該股票的價格約為 44 美元，而且支付了不錯的股息（ 1.8 美元/股，約 4%）。

您認為我應該把股票賣掉嗎？

作為投資者，我通常會盡可能長時間持股，尤其是股息不錯的情況。在某些時候，我需要重新平衡投資組合，才會考慮出售股票。

例如，我曾經在一家製藥公司工作，分到了很多股票，作為我工資的一部分。突然間，我發現整個投資組合的 50% 都在這隻股票上。風險太大了，我得分散投資以減少風險。

健康和財務

假設該公司股價為 120 美元。我沒有直接出售股票，而是以 120 美元的執行價格出售了 5 份為期 1 個月的 CALL 期權合約。溢價為 3.4 美元/股。一個月後，該股票上漲至每股 122 美元。我被迫以 120 美元的價格賣出 500 股。然而，實際上我的出售價是 123.4 美元/股。

問題來了。那一年，資本收益使我的所得稅跳了一級。

之前我強調過，所有的一切，包括我的生命，都只是暫時託付給我的。我的責任就是按照神的帶領好好使用它們。上帝提醒我，由於計劃不周而付了很多稅，顯然沒有管理好祂託付給我的資產。祷告之後，我找到了一種更好的方法來重新平衡投資組合：將股票捐贈給教会或非營利基督教機構。

如果你考慮所得稅問題，而且每年有定期捐贈，那麼試著設立一個捐贈者衍生的慈善基金，並在今年捐贈多一些。您可以獲得稅收減免。還可以在未來幾年從該基金中捐款。

關於交易期權的附加說明。

首先，要做期權交易，您需要開一個經紀保證金賬戶。 有了保證金賬戶，您可以借錢投資股票。 但千萬不要借錢進行投資。只有當您有多餘的現金可支配時，才考慮投資股票市場。

其次，我曾經提到了我的財政學教授的評論，在此重申一下：美國市場非常高效率。 當您收到一條新聞時，可能大多數人已經都知道了。 因此，不要相信其他人告訴您要買賣哪個股票或期權的信息。 必須自己進行研究而後得出結論。 當然您可以閱讀其他人對您感興趣的股票/期權的看法， 但請對他人的觀點持保留態度。

第三點，我提過 我的教授的另一個建議。 在任何給定時間，資金池都是固定的。 當一個人虧錢時，必定有另一個人賺錢。如果您想賺錢，去弄清楚誰經常賠錢，然後做相反的事情。

由於時間這因素，交易期權比股票複雜許多。 當您購買股票時，就擁有該公司的一部分，並且在您出售股票前，您對該公司的所有權不會過期。　期權是不同的，因為它不是所有權而是合同。　當合同時間到了，您的期權就變得毫無用處。

許多網站宣傳您可以通過期權交易（主要是購買期權）獲得每週 5% 的回報。　然而，根據股票平台 Etoro 的數據，80% 的日常交易者一年內平均虧損額為 36.3%。　華爾街和其他消息來源估計，90% 的投資者在購買期權時會賠錢。

事實上，大多數購買期權的人都會在合約到期時損失期權費（溢價）。　為了賺錢，做相反的事情，那就是出售(而非購買)期權。

第四點，不要試圖出售裸期權（即在不擁有股票的情況下出售看漲期權，或在沒有現金的情況下出售看跌期權），因為您可能陷入在期權到期時無法履行義務的困境。　裸期權違背了風險與收益平衡的原則。

儘管不同的期權交易策略（例如，蝶式價差、跨式期權⋯⋯）看起來很誘人，但我堅持自己的方法，使用期權作為買賣股票的工具。　因此，賣看跌期權時，我留備現金，感興趣的股票若價格跌破我賣出期權的執行價，就買入該股票。　我只出售備兌看漲期權（亦即我擁有該股票）。

記得有一次我在教會與某人分享了我的投資策略，一個月後，他向我匯報了情況。　「你的策略行不通。　我被迫借錢購買了 1000 股 XXX 股票。」

我回答：「我從來沒有借錢買過股票。」

同一個人後來又犯了另一個錯誤。「我按照你的策略，賣出了三份看跌期權合約來購買 ZZZ 股票。　你猜怎麼了？　我現在手裡握著 300 股毫無價值的股票。」

我問他：「你研究過 ZZZ 並得出結論想長期持有這家公司的一部分嗎？」

他撓了撓頭。　「一位朋友告訴我，ZZZ 剛剛在非洲發現了一個大金礦。　我認為值得博一博。」

健康和財務

　　拜託，別想賭博。　好好進行股票分析，管理上帝託付給您的一切，成为一位值得信賴的管家。

路得

第十四章：資產配置與不動產

「不要把所有的雞蛋都放在一個籃子裡。」

　　是的，大多數人都聽說過這句諺語。背後的哲學是什麼？即盡可能降低失去所有財產的風險。

　　資產配置旨在幫您將辛苦得來的雞蛋放入不同的籃子來平衡風險和回報。可惜找不到一個通用的簡單公式，因為每個人都有不同的目標、風險承受能力、和投資期限。

　　三種主要資產類別——股票、固定收益、現金及等價物——各具有不同水平的風險和回報。一般來說，風險越高，回報就越好。

　　如果你明年需要 20,000 美元買一輛新車，可能不應該把錢投入股市。即使銀行利率超低，至少在需要錢購買車時，您可以提款套現。

　　這個簡單的例子說明了關鍵點：仔細分析您當前和未來的情況，相應地制定投資策略。

　　當然，沒有人能預測未來。利率可升可跌，股票會波動。當利率上升時，成長型股票的吸引力就會下降。投資理財確實不容易。歸根結底，人的生命在上帝的手中，我們的責任是計劃

健康和財務

許多書籍和文章都提供了關於資產配置的建議：為緊急情況留些現金、60/40（60% 股票/40% 債券）公式等。因此，我不會深入探討這些的細節，只想分享 2008 年房地產市場崩盤後，我如何將資金轉到房子上。

買低賣高。這原則不只適用於股市，是的，其他投資一樣用得到。但是我怎麼知道市場已經達到了最低点呢？

確實沒有一定的方法可以抓住最低點，但是，當市場呈螺旋式下降，每個人都在撤離時，這是採取行動的明顯信號。

我饒有興趣地看著房地產泡沫的破滅。 2009 年底，我查看了銀行的利率后告訴老公：「這是我們千載難逢的機會。現在將一些錢投入房地產，可以獲得更好的回報。」

去舊金山出差期間，我查看了 Zillow.com，發現東灣的一所銀行因屋住付不出房貸收回自行出售的房屋標價 260,000 美元。幾年前，這所房子的售價為 580,000 美元。

我打電話給一位当經紀的朋友，晚上去看了房子。一個月之後，我們用自己住屋為抵押的房屋淨值貸款買下它。

回到芝加哥，我們找到類似的一家銀行自行出售的公寓標價 140,000 美元。我要求經紀人提供出 94,000 美元的現金報價，銀行接受了。

僅在 2010 年，我們購入了四間出租物業。

當然，做房東是一項艱苦的工作，並不適合所有人。我們聘請了物業經理來管理這四個物業，租金扣除各樣費用後，回報仍然優於銀行利率。

東灣的那棟房子後来所麼樣了呢？幾年來它的價值節節高升，我們在 2021 年將它捐贈給了慈善剩餘信託基金。

也許在不久的將來另一個泡沫又破滅，那將是另一個資產配置的機會。

第十五章：創業

您是否曾經夢想成為自己的老闆，如此就可以規劃每一天的時間表並賺取可觀的收入？

Dragomir Simovic 於 2022 年 7 月 28 日發表的一篇文章有以下的統計數據：

* 90% 的美國新晉億萬富翁都是白手起家。

* 2016 年，有 2500 萬美國人開始或已經擁有自己的企業。

* 企業失敗的首要原因是什麼？ 產品缺乏市場需求。

* 46% 的小企業主年齡在 41 到 56 歲之間。

* 全球有 5.82 億企業家。

* 百分之二十的小企業在第一年就倒閉了。

* 研究表明，中年男性創辦的企業成功率最高。

在亞馬遜搜索框中鍵入「創業」一词，將彈出 60,000 多本書。 我不想重複那些書的信息，而是想分享自己的經驗。

第一階段：規劃

當前雇主取消我的項目並將我調到另一個部門時，我萌生了發新藥，針対治療慢性腎病的併發症， 然而，我的公司却退出了腎病藥物領域。我堅信繼續努力下去最終會幫助許多患者。

由於在工作過的大型製藥公司，我曾參與過廣泛的市場調查，對市場和競爭有一定程度的認知。 過往的經歷還讓我充分了解到開發新藥所需的成本、和面対的風險和挑戰。

但我沒有立即辭職，而是讓我的想法擱置了兩年。 經過多次禱告後，我制定了一份商業計劃书並辭去了工作。

第二階段：啟動

第一步，很簡單，就是註冊我的公司。

下一步，獲得資金，就困難得多。 那時，我們擁有創意、專業知識、和經驗等無形資產。 但沒有專利或任何有形的東西來吸引投資者。 通過專業上的關係，我找到了幾位有相同理念的天使投資人（為小企業提供資金以換取股權的富有私人投資者）。 籌得 600,000 美元的資金之后，我們建了一個實驗室開始臨床前研究。

第三階段：維持及前進

任何曾在生物科技領域工作過的人都知曉科學研究燒錢的速度有多快。 我們精打細算。 儘管如此，初始資金在不到一年的時間裡就燒光了。 幸運的是，我們最初合成的幾種化合物測試均有好結果。 有了這些數據，我們申請了 NIH SBIR（美國國立衛生研究院小企業創新研究）資助。

長話短說，我們收到了 6 筆 NIH 撥款，並從投資者那裡籌集了另兩輪資金。 這筆錢使公司能夠將我們的化合物由動物實驗推進臨床人體研究。

第四階段：退出

十年後，公司的一些最初投資者顯得有些焦躁不安。 他們什麼時候才能得到投資回報？

從一項針對 10 名腎病透析患者的臨床研究中，我們取得了出色的數據。 下一步是二期臨床，需要大約 2000 萬美元在

200 多名患者身上評估該化合物的效用。 我們有辦法找到那么多錢嗎？

經過多次討論，公司的董事會做出了決定，將該項目賣給了一家風險投資公司。 因為沒有二期臨床研究的數據，無法賺取超過 2 億美元，而是根據現有數據以低十倍的價格出售。

好在最初的投資者都已欣喜若狂，因為他們得到了十倍以上的回報。

以我自己的故事為例，告誡大家，如果你有興趣成為一名企業家，請在辭職前仔細研究上述四個階段。

您必須估算當前職位與新工作之間的收入淨差。 就我而言，在收到 NIH 資助之前，公司付我的工資是期權而不是現金。 我在規劃過程中就做好了準備，我們一家靠丈夫的收入和家里的投資收益撐了好幾年。

規劃的另一個重要部分是分析新業務運營的盈虧平衡點。 不要因對潛在收益過於樂觀而低估成本和風險。 由於在生物科技方面進行這種分析非常困難，我告訴所有的投資者，他們投資損失不見的可能性超過 95%。

最後重要的一點是，缺乏相關行業經驗的情況下， 切勿辭職創業。 對於企業家來說，培訓和專業知識絕對至關重要。 如果沒有我的科研背景和多年的新藥研發經驗，我的小公司不會引起天使投資人的興趣。

第十六章：退休及財產規劃

「優雅地老去」這個詞在嬰兒潮一代中似乎很流行。它意味著「雖有變老的跡象，但仍在向前邁進」。 對我來說，與其悲嘆已進入国家醫療保險(Medicare)的年齡，不如為仍然活着來感谢上帝的祝福。 我的許多朋友都沒有机会變老就走了。

我的另一半曾舉辦的很受歡迎的研討會題目是「再愛他們一次」，關於如何管理你生命最後一程的詼諧演講。

怎样做才能在年老時不給所愛的人施加不必要的負擔呢？ 以下是一些重點。

（1）退休時仍持有生命目標

如果您在亞馬遜搜索框中輸入「退休」一詞，超過 70,000個結果立即跳出來。 如何讓儲蓄步入正軌，何時領取社會保險，以及如何弄妥醫療保健……從退休規劃指南到退休時要做的1001 件有趣的事情，眾多好書隨您挑選。

我不想在這裡重覆那些話題，而是分享我們的個人經驗。

每个人都期待著不用去辦公室報到，可以全年休假那一天早日到來。 幾年前，我們終於等到那一天了。

集中

路得

經過幾十年的工作，我和另一半第一次不必遵循緊湊的時間表。 每天的感覺都一樣， 星期五也不再帶來興奮。 長周末嗎？不用說了， 所有的周末對我們來說都太長了。

日曆中沒有任何必須要做的事，也缺乏結構。

在去了兩次長假之後，無聊感迎面襲來。我們得找些事幹。

不，我們不能像在遊輪上遇到的那位紳士， 在同一艘船上度過 26 週。不停地旅行會讓我們抓狂。

應該報名參加更多的志願者工作嗎？ 我們不想找些亂七八糟的活動來消磨時間，而是需要目標和方向——來自上帝的新任務，繼續在祂的國度中效力。

一位朋友提前退休，去國外當傳教士。這是一種可能，但應該還有其他吧？

經過一番禱告尋求，終於找到了上帝要我們做的事。

然而，每個人的方式都不一樣。 關鍵是為您的退休生活禱告，讓聖靈引導您人生最後一程的全新探險。

（2）授權書（Powers of Attorney, POA）、長期護理保險

如果我夠幸運，可能会活到大腦不再能正常運作的年齡。 到時需要另一個人為我的重大事件做決定。 這就是 POA 發揮作用的時候。

POA 是一份法律文件，允許其他人為我們做財務或醫療決定。一般來說，我們需要兩份 POA，一份用於財務，另一份用於醫療保健。 這兩者之間， 有一些細微差別，通過在線搜索，您可以輕鬆找到更多信息。

應該購買長期護理保險嗎？ 值得嗎？ 根據社區生活管理局的說法，一名 65 歲的人在不久的將來有 70% 的機會需要某種類型的長期護理。 2021 年，家庭健康助理的中位數一年費用為 61,776 美元，療養院私人房間的中位數一年費用為 108,405 美元。 如果您是超級富家或非常貧窮(後者有政府醫療補助

Medicaid)，都可以不用擔心。 然而，對於大多數中產階級來說，購買保單是一個明智的決定。 就像醫療保險政策一樣，應該在您還健康的時候購買。 如果早開始，支付保費的時間比較長，但費率會相對便宜，而且可以終身鎖定該保費。

盼望這些信息對您有幫助。

財產規劃又是怎么一回事呢？

(1) 可撤銷生前信託

顧名思義，可撤銷生前信託是可以隨時更改的。 它們有助於免除遺囑認證、可以減少遺產稅、以及保護您和受益人的隱私。但是，缺點是您必須聘請律師起草文件，並且還需要每年進行監控並根據需要加以調整。 此外，您必須在退休賬戶指定受益人，並為所有非退休賬戶制定死亡轉移的指示。

上述段落目的不是要提供所有信息，而是要提您注意這課題，盼望您進行更多研究加以規劃。

(2) 慈善剩餘信託 （CRT）

如前所述，2009 年，我带着興致，冷眼旁观房地產泡沫的破滅。 在去舊金山出差期間，查看 Zillow.com 之時，我發現東灣一棟銀行拿回的房子標價 26 萬 美元。 幾年前，那所房子以 58 萬美元的價格售出。 我打電話給一位經紀人朋友，在晚上參觀了房子。 一個月後，我們以自住的房子為抵押申請房屋淨值貸款，購買了那所房產。

2021 年，我丈夫退休後，我們決定賣掉那所房子，以減少在房地產的投資。

可是有一嚴重的問題。 那房子的價值增加了很多，如果我們賣掉它，要納的稅是一筆極大的數目。

在那段時間裡，我們每天都為此事禱告。 一次偶然的機會，我看到一篇關於慈善剩餘信託 （CRT）， 或稱为慈善剩餘年金信託 （CRAT），的文章。我對這課題並不熟悉。 經過更多的研究什麼是 CRT 或 CRAT？ 來自維基百科的定義如下：

「慈善剩餘年金信託（CRAT）是一種計劃捐贈工具. 首先，捐贈者將大量現金或財產贈與信託。 然後，信託每年支付固定數額的收入給捐贈人或捐贈人指定的受益人。 當捐贈者去世時，信託的剩餘部分則轉移給慈善機構。 CRAT 等慈善信託需要受託人。 有時慈善機構被命名為受託人，有時則是第三方，例如律師、銀行或財務顧問。」

然而，維基百科上的信息並非完全準確。 我們所設立的是一個 20 年的 CRT，意味著信託的剩餘部分將在 20 年後轉移到指定的慈善機構，無論我們是否還活著。 如果我們在 CRT 期間死亡，那麼CRT會自動進入我們的可撤銷生前信託（見上文）。此外，我和丈夫沒有指定他人作為受託人，而是自己擔任 CRT 的受託人。

請注意，CRT 不可撤銷且極為複雜。 您必須聘請一位優秀的律師才能正確完成。 通過選擇的三個慈善組織之一，我們認識一位傑出的基督徒律師，在整個過程中順利地建立了我们的CRT。

(3) 其他財產規劃的提醒

以下段落來自我們的朋友 Ronald Tollerud，他在三一國際大學擔任計劃捐贈和特殊禮物主任。

「財產規劃的主要目標是確保您的財富在您希望的時間以您希望的形式轉移到您所揀選的人和組織。 次要目標是有計劃地轉移以盡量減少稅收和其他費用。」

然而，大多數美國人並不考慮財產規劃。 經過一生的工作和積累財富，最終，大多數人將死後如何處置財產的決定權交給國家法律。

作為基督徒，我們應該將一切視為是託付給自己暫時保管的。財產規劃是我們努力成為上帝的好管家和投資永恆的重要一步。

所以，隨著年齡的增長，做我們需要做的事情。 做好您的財產規劃，拋開煩惱，朝着天家邁去。

第十七章：結論

假如一百萬——1,000,000——象徵您的生命，如果那個「一」完好無損，所有的各種機會才得以實現。

請記住：我們的健康是那個「一」，後面跟著許多零。 沒有那個「一」，所有的「零」都毫無意義。

我之前提到過，健康、財富、和人際關係是相互交織關聯的，很難將其中任何一個單獨拿出來討論。 身為一名基督徒企業家，解讀健康、財務、和人際關係之間的密切聯繫是我一生的追求。

我在這本小冊子中沒有涉及的一個領域是人際關係。 其實我故意不討論那課題，因為那是個永久也談不完的題目。

我和先生符合「異性相吸」的理論。 他是夜貓子，而我是個早起鳥。 他是典型B型性格，輕鬆、耐心、隨和，當他達不到目標時只輕嘆口氣，不會感到具大壓力。 而我，是典型的 A 型人格，持續地、緊迫地鞭策自己努力實現目標，常常置平衡的生活於不顧。

在四十多年的美好婚姻中，神如何在我們身上作工，使我們不僅相處融洽，而且幫助彼此達到身體、金錢、人際關係的平衡？ 靠著主的憐憫，也許在下一本小冊子中，我可以分享更多

和 人 際 關 係 的 想 法 。　 請 隨 時 在 我 的 網 站
(www.ruthforchrist.com) 上 給 我 留 言。

***

如何實行：依下面的例子来制定您的實施計劃。　如果能依此格
式在各方面有行動，也許得以改善您的健康和財務狀況。

例一

目的：養成每天運動的習慣

目標：在六個月內實現可見/可衡量的變化

評估過程：每週檢查一次，看看您的新習慣是否堅持下來。

成功的證據：六個月後，檢查您的目標是否取得了可見/可衡
量的改變（例如，是否体重減輕等）

結果/成就：

時間軸	要做的事情	親友的支援
第 1 步（第 1 週）：	寫下您所期望的健康狀況。	與信任的親友一起檢查您的清單。
第 2 步（第 2 週）：	重讀第3章，檢查您的日常生活並鎖定一個「習慣循環」——觸發器（或提示）、例行程序、和獎勵。	與信任的親友分享第3章.
第 3 步（第 3 週）：	在您的日常活動中添加一項易於進行的運動（例如十個仰臥起坐），而不改變提示和獎勵。	與信賴的親友分享您新有的習慣。
第 4 步（第 4 - 7 週）：	繼續努力。	每周至少一次與親友分享您的進展。
第 5 步（第 8 週）：	在您的日常活動中添加另一項易於進行的運動（例如，伸展三分鐘）。	與信賴的親友分享您新修改的習慣。
第 9 週及以後：	重複步驟 1-5。	享受全新的您。

評估過程：檢查新習慣是否堅持下來。

成功的證據：六個月後，檢查您是否實現了目標（例如，減肥
、感覺更有活力等）

作者感謝的話

謝謝您選讀了这书。 如果您有時間，请帮忙写下书评， 感謝您的協助。

有兴趣的话，请查看作者以筆名 R. F. Whong 撰寫的小說。

作者簡介

路得獲得了正道神學院 （https://www.les.edu）的基督教研究碩士學位，俄亥俄州立大學生物化學博士學位，和伊利諾伊州立大學金融工商管理碩士。

她在一家小型生物技術公司 工作，過去幾年為該公司籌集了超過 2000 萬美元。她發表了 120 多篇科學論文和書籍（使用法定全名）以及一些非科學書籍/文章（以路得的筆名寫作）。

她與丈夫住在美國中西部，丈夫是一名退休牧師，1987 年至 2020 年間在三間教會事奉。他們的兒子已成年，在附近的城市工作。

想與她聯繫吗？请到 www.ruthforchrist.com.

Made in the USA
Middletown, DE
05 October 2023

39997507R00071